17.   £2.99

GW00538090

The Cinema of
E R N S T
L U B I T S C H:

The Hollywood Films

The Cinema of
ERNST LUBITSCH

Leland A. Poague

Filmography by Gary Hooper *and* Leland A. Poague

SOUTH BRUNSWICK AND NEW YORK: A. S. BARNES AND COMPANY
LONDON: THOMAS YOSELOFF LTD

© 1978 by A.S. Barnes and Co., Inc.

A.S. Barnes and Co., Inc.
Cranbury, New Jersey 08512

The Tantivy Press
Magdalen House
136-148 Tooley Street
London SE1 2TT, England

Library of Congress Cataloging in Publication Data

Poague, Leland A   1948-
  The cinema of Ernst Lubitsch.

  Bibliography: p.
  Filmography: p.
  Includes index.
  1. Lubitsch, Ernst, 1892-1947. I. Title.
PN1998.A3L837   791.43'0233'0924   76-18481
ISBN 0-498-01958-6

Contents

Ernst Lubitsch: always the master.

Preface

Readers familiar with *The Cinema of Frank Capra* are doubtless aware of my general approach to the task of film criticism: I tend to emphasise close analysis rather than casual value judgements, detailed scholarship rather than haphazard evaluation, and the films themselves rather than the memorabilia of film production.

The present volume abides by these general principles. Yet its genesis dictates a certain practical limitation on comprehensiveness. This essay on Ernst Lubitsch began as a chapter in a multi-director book on film authorship and Hollywood comedy. The essay as eventually written, however, grew in length so far beyond the original limits that publishing it as a book in its own right became the only practical alternative to cutting it down.

Thus my decision not to discuss *Madame Dubarry,* for example, ought not to be interpreted as a value judgement. No doubt *Madame Dubarry* and the other German films are well worth attending to. But even had I decided to include Lubitsch's German work in this study, comprehensiveness of the ideal sort would have been impossible: too many Lubitsch films (both German and American) are lost to allow a complete history. I never intended, therefore, to be exhaustive: I rather sought to be representative and suggestive. Thus, despite the limitations of this study, I believe that I understand Lubitsch more thoroughly than he has been understood before. Indeed, twenty-eight of his forty-odd feature films were made in Hollywood, and it does not seem presumptuous to suppose that a detailed examination of Lubitsch's American period will mark a positive advance in Lubitsch scholarship.

My orientation, then, is auteurist — and while I will define what that particular notion requires of critical discourse in the chapters which follow, a few brief observations and qualifications are in order.

Ernst Lubitsch (right) with C. B. DeMille.

First of all, auteurism, as I understand it, is not concerned with creation *per se* but with expression. Expressiveness, of course, is a natural corollary to creation; and it is therefore tempting to assume that each entails the other — which is certainly true to a point. It is clear, however, that film-making is a collaborative enterprise, that no one man alone could possibly "create" a film like *Ninotchka*. Nevertheless, to admit the collaborative nature of film-making in no way denies the possibility that a certain personality or viewpoint may come to dominate production, may actually serve to orchestrate individual contributions towards a certain aesthetic or expressive end. Indeed, as auteurist scholarship has repeatedly and effectively demonstrated, such is very frequently the case; and the person most often responsible for dictating the logic by which disparate contributions are brought together is the director.

8

Auteurism, then, is not a natural law but a working hypothesis, a provisional assumption that any given film can *best* be understood in the context of its director's career. Directorial continuity is important, therefore, not as a yardstick for quick value-judgements, but for providing a fruitful paradigm which more readily permits understanding. The more we know in general about Ernst Lubitsch, the greater our awareness of his characteristic themes and concerns, then the more likely we are to understand and appreciate the next Lubitsch film we see. In other words, knowledge begets knowledge, and the more we bring to a work of art the more we are likely to get back in return.

It is unfortunate, therefore, that auteurist discourse tends to dwell almost obsessively upon the issue of attribution, as if that were the end of study rather than the means. Ultimately, it matters very little whether we assign sole authorship of *One Hour with You,* for instance, to Lubitsch (who produced it and signed it) or to George Cukor (who directed sections of it under Lubitsch's supervision). What matters is that we find the film a vital aesthetic experience and that we use appropriate conceptual tools to come to terms with that experience. It seems clear to me on the basis of my familiarity with both Lubitsch and Cukor that *One Hour with You* can be usefully discussed as a Lubitsch film, and I have done so. Doing so, however, does not deny that another scholar, under other circumstances, might find it interesting to discuss *One Hour with You* as a Cukor film: it depends on the frame of reference. The point to keep in mind, however, is that the phrase "the cinema of" must always be understood as an extremely powerful and useful generalisation, certainly accurate within its limits, indispensable, it seems to me, for any real understanding of cinema, but incapable of accounting for every vagary of the movie-making business.

Acknowledgments

My thanks are due first to Peter Cowie. Without his encouragement I would not have written this book. Thanks are also due to Paul Stein and William Rueckert for their support of the Geneseo film study program. Jim Garvey, Mr. and Mrs. James Garvey, Frank Hendricks, and Jon and Carol Sanford are to be thanked for their hospitality. Film showings were arranged with the assistance of Liz Ancker and the SUNY Geneseo Instructional Resources Center, Marshall Deutelbaum and James Card of George Eastman House, Barbara Humphrys and the Library of Congress Motion Picture Section staff, Charles Silver and the Museum of Modern Art Film Study Center, and William K. Everson. Gary Hooper and Dante Thomas read and commented on the manuscript — I am very grateful for their advice. I am also grateful to my wife, Susan, for her editorial advice and typing skill. Stills appear through the courtesy and assistance of George Pratt and the George Eastman House staff (special thanks to Nancy), and Paula Klaw of "Movie Star News." I would also like to acknowledge a general debt to the writings of Robin Wood and Andrew Sarris, and to the teachings of William Cadbury. Finally, thanks to the gang at the Bijou — it always helps to view films with friends.

This book is dedicated to
Robert and Leone Sanford

Introduction

Ernst Lubitsch is generally remembered for his cinematic wit, for his gracefully charming and fluid style, for his ingenious ability to suggest more than he showed and to show more than others dared suggest; for all of those qualities and characteristics known collectively as "The Lubitsch Touch." The phrase is certainly memorable, and it does a fair enough job of summarising the most immediately striking aspects of the Lubitsch cinema. But unfortunately, it leads to a rather unedifying, though pleasant, sort of reportage. Herman G. Weinberg's *The Lubitsch Touch,* for example, seldom goes beyond the level of assertion, as if Weinberg's generalisations, developed through the course of an informal Lubitsch biography, were self-evidently true. They may be true to a degree, but merely listing instances of particular cinematic ingenuity seems ultimately a disservice both to the films and their director.

I do not necessarily mean to slight Weinberg's work: check-lists such as his are delightful in their way — particularly as they spark our recollections — and there can be little doubt that Lubitsch himself took great, almost child-like pleasure in his powers to amuse and amaze. Lubitsch, indeed, was a crown prince in Hollywood's kingdom of fantasy; and therefore it is no coincidence that two of his great pre-occupations were privilege and imagination. That much is clear from reading Weinberg, however sketchy his account may be.

Yet, despite his privileged position, Lubitsch never lost a strong sense of humanity, a strong sense of empathy for people and their problems. Thus, for all of his concern with the surfaces and routines of human existence, Lubitsch was equally concerned with the emotional realities beneath the facades of frivolity. Indeed, the movement of a typical Lubitsch film involves the stripping away of such facades and their

13

reconstitution in more humane and self-aware forms. Life cannot function without some measure of routine, or so Lubitsch demonstrates in his films, but routine can become so encrusted and entrenched as to endanger life rather than preserve it. Hence the necessity that we keep perception and convention in balance.

A similar movement — in the direction of greater self-awareness, a

Masks and disguises: Pola Negri in *Sumurun.*

deeper understanding of the human condition — characterises the entire Lubitsch canon. As his career and his vision developed, Lubitsch relied less and less on visual razzle-dazzle. His famous "touch" evolved into a more catholic vision of life's problems and priorities. Lubitsch became less concerned with asserting his own cinematic ingenuity than with exploring the humanity of his characters. Of course, Lubitsch did not abandon his concern for artifice, but the artifice in the later films is more a function of the characters themselves, of their often ludicrous need for masks and disguises (e.g. *To Be or Not to Be*). In other words,

14

Lubitsch shifted his focus from the edges of the frame, those artificial boundaries which allowed him to leave things out, to the centre of the frame, that privileged area where the human comedy is enacted. The logic of development in Lubitsch's American films is thus consistent in its broad outlines, from men's manners to men's hearts, from the edges to the centre, from the surface to the substance. Examining *The Marriage Circle* and *The Shop Around the Corner* will clarify the point.

The Cinema of
E R N S T
L U B I T S C H:

The Hollywood Films

1 Time and the Man: The Marriage Circle (1924) and The Shop Around the Corner (1940)

The Marriage Circle was Lubitsch's second American film, made immediately after the Lubitsch/Mary Pickford *Rosita,* and it was the first of Lubitsch's "social comedies," as Theodore Huff termed them, that sequence of films from *The Marriage Circle* to *So This Is Paris* in which Lubitsch explored the serio-comic aspects of the marital estate.[1] Indeed, *The Marriage Circle* initiates this investigation by focusing on two distinctively different though potentially similar marriages. The first, representing a world of hedonistic experience, is the marriage of Mizzi and Josef Stock. Theirs is a long established and self-destructive relationship, based more on mutual distaste than mutual trust. At some level they respect each other — both are old hands at the game of reciprocal bad manners — but antagonism has clearly overcome affection.

Contrasting with this relationship is the newly-solemnised marriage of Charlotte and Dr. Franz Braun. Both are innocents who somehow manage to retain their innocence despite the bizarre sequence of emotional misfortunes which befall them. At the height of their mutual antagonism, when their sense of alienation is at its greatest, their actions and reactions remain essentially child-like; they feel shame far out of proportion to the offence (and Franz's offence, allowing Mizzi's heavy-duty attentions to fan momentarily the fires of his masculine vanity, has an adolescent quality to it), and fear far out of proportion to the apparent danger (Charlotte really does believe, at Mizzi's urging,

19

Lubitsch directs Mary Pickford in *Rosita*.

that Franz has fallen for Mlle. Hofer, when in fact Franz is doing his bumbling best to avoid Mizzi's entangling schemes). Even at the end of the film when Charlotte tells Franz, "I'm as guilty as you," there is little sense that she understands how that might actually be true. On the contrary, she says it not as an admission of folly (as Gerald Mast argues) but as a trick to keep her husband's attentions from ever wandering again.[2]

Quite frankly, I am not at all sure that Franz and Charlotte really do learn any lesson for their experience. By chance they are caught up in a potentially disastrous crisis of mistaken motives and mistaken identities, and it is only by chance (i.e. their coincidental meeting in Mizzi's hotel room) that they are enabled to escape the consequences. If their marriage is one of "perfect happiness," as Charlotte describes it to

Mizzi, then marriage at its best is only an elaborate and cyclical game of blind man's bluff.

Far more interesting, and ultimately far more disturbing, is the Mizzi/Professor Stock relationship. The film opens in their bedroom, and the scene is worth considering in some detail for what it reveals (and does not reveal) about their marriage in particular and about the film's concerns in general.

The day (which we discover is a working day) "starts late but gloriously in the home of Prof. Josef Stock." The Professor sits on the edge of his bed (we see only his feet) and attempts to put on his left sock. He gets it on well enough, but his big toe protrudes rather prominently through a very conspicuous hole. The issue of domestic neglect is thus raised, and is refined when a shrewish Mizzi rather disgustedly picks up a pile of the Professor's clothes from a chair and tosses them on to the bed. The Professor then gets up, and the cause of his sartorial frustration is revealed. His dresser drawer is empty save for a rather forlorn collection of stiff celluloid collars (the issues of rigidity and propriety). Mizzi then enters the shot, and nonchalantly shrugs her shoulders as if to plead innocence (she had no idea he was sockless). She closes his drawer, opens her own — a drawer full to bursting with stockings neatly arranged in rows (issues of self-indulgence and self-control) — and she takes out a pair to put on. She walks over to the bed to do so and sits down, but only after tossing the piled clothes back on to the chair.

The Professor, meanwhile, maintains a determined, dead-pan expression, and he walks across the room as if nothing had happened. He hangs a small mirror from the window-frame and proceeds to lather up for shaving (the issue of appearance). Mizzi, however, must fix her hair, so she takes the mirror from the window and walks back across the room to the dresser, where she turns and stands, the small mirror held out in front, her back to the mirror on top of the dressing-table. The Professor smiles (one of those marvellous Adolphe Menjou smiles, all cheeks and moustache) and decides it's time to get back into bed. Mizzi takes this as an affront, and berates his laziness. The Professor just rolls over and hides his head in the pillow. She leaves the room, he throws back the covers, swings his legs out of bed, sighs the sigh of a patient man, and smiles after her. He then gets up, goes over to the pulley apparatus on the far wall, and begins his morning calisthenics.

Mizzi, meanwhile, completes her toilet with the aid of two maids, one of whom brings her a note:

Dearest Mizzi:
    I just learned that you moved to Vienna two months ago, and I

feel hurt that you didn't let me know. I'm so anxious to see you again and have you meet my husband. You and your husband must call soon.

Affectionately,
Charlotte.

Mizzi seems genuinely pleased by the letter, excited at the prospect of seeing her old friend, and she takes the note into the bedroom to show it to the Professor. He reads it unemotionally, and goes back to his exercises, turning his back to Mizzi as he squats up and down (and in and out of the frame). Mizzi is annoyed, and tells him: "Keep on with your cruelty and some day I'll leave you." The Professor stops, turns around, raises his arm in a gesture of resignation, and smiles. The smile clearly indicates that Mizzi's departure would be welcomed (the Professor eventually hires a detective to gather evidence for divorce proceedings). Mizzi only sneers and replies: "That's just what you want — but you'll not get rid of me so easily." The Professor only turns away and looks in mock-solemnity off into the distance. Mizzi begins to leave, but she pokes her head back through the door to say something. Again, the Professor does not respond, except to continue his exercises, thrusting his posterior in her direction.

There are several notable things about the scene, not the least of which is the ingenuity with which Lubitsch describes the sequence of events, but surely the most striking aspect of the sequence is its studied formality — for every insult there is a counter-insult, for every move a counter-move. Things happen twice: twice the clothes are tossed from bed to chair (or back again), twice the drawers are opened, twice the mirror is carried across the room. It's as if the scene were well rehearsed, daily enacted, a pattern of behaviour so familiar as to provide, in its familiarity, a certain sense of security, although it is a security based on the certainty of mutual antagonism. Like the rest of the film, then, this scene is a game played by certain rules, the most fundamental being that a player should never lose control. Mizzi comes close here, by threatening to leave, but that is just what the Professor wants and Mizzi catches herself. She's not about to give in to him. Furthermore, when played expertly, the game can be rewarding to a point. The Professor's frequent smiles indicate not only pleasure with his own moves, but admiration for Mizzi's stratagems as well.

We learn something about the Charlotte/Franz relationship also. Charlotte's note to Mizzi indicates, at the very least, Charlotte's concern for the niceties of feeling (her "hurt" at Mizzi's silence), her pride, verging on anxiety, in her marriage and her husband, and her desire to measure her marriage against the general norm (she invites

Mizzi *and* the Professor). In other words, Charlotte sees herself as living an idealised existence (otherwise she would hardly get so upset at her husband's failure to take some roses she had given him to the office). Charlotte's devotion to the ideal makes it all the more easy for game-players of Mizzi's calibre to exploit her *naivète*. Franz and

Monte Blue and Marie Prevost in *The Marriage Circle.*

Charlotte are both, after all, relatively passive. They do not so much act as react. The real "actors" in the film are the Professor, as evidenced in the opening scene, and Mizzi, whose elaborate scheme to seduce Franz almost succeeds, and certainly succeeds well enough — at least in terms of its superficial manifestations (i.e. Franz's midnight visit to Mizzi) — to provide the Professor with sufficient grounds for divorce. As the Professor tells Franz, after Franz pleads his innocence to the charge of romancing Mizzi: "I believe you, but nobody else will."

But the real difficulty with *The Marriage Circle* is not so much what happens as why. To put it briefly, there is no real sense of motive behind the shared antagonism of Mizzi and Professor Stock. We assume, I believe, that their marriage started on the right foot, as a genuine expression of trust, affection, and shared goals, which somewhere along the line went sour and degenerated to the point of game-playing. Mizzi clearly no longer harbours any affection for her husband. The first of their two embraces is only a ruse which allows Mizzi to kick her empty

Mizzi (Marie Prevost) and Professor Stock (Adolphe Menjou).

pistol (Mizzi had threatened "suicide" in an attempt to frighten Franz) under the table, out of the Professor's sight; and she hides evidence of infidelity not for the purpose of really patching things up but rather to avoid divorce and financial hardship. Their second embrace, only moments later as they sit on the divan in Mizzi's sitting room, is similarly intended to avoid divorce rather than re-kindle genuine concern. The Professor's feelings for Mizzi are only slightly more ambiguous. Generally speaking, he is as ruthless as she, but he clearly admires her ingenuity, and there is a moment when past affection is reflected in present action.

Mizzi literally kisses up to the Professor, hopping into his lap as they sit on the divan; but her little girl routine is interrupted by the door-bell (rung, it turns out, by the detective). Mizzi gets up to answer the door; and the Professor, left alone, slowly passes his hand over the couch, where Mizzi had been sitting, as if to recapture for a moment her warmth. Lubitsch does not dwell on this gesture, nor does he trivialise

The Lubitsch vamp circa 1918: Pola Negri as *Carmen.*

it by resorting to unnecessary close-ups. He simply observes, and the observation in itself is eloquent.

At some point, then, Mizzi and the Professor probably mattered to each other, as Charlotte and Franz certainly matter to one another at the film's beginning. But Mizzi and the Professor let something come between them, we do not know what, and they then began their daily ceremony of abusiveness; and the ritual became so powerful, as it grew in scope and intensity, that the reasons behind the ritual were forgotten. Time has a way, therefore, of magnifying even the most petty differences far beyond their original significance. Thus it seems legitimate to conclude that the antipathy between Mizzi and the Professor had its roots in something no more important than a few forgotten roses. Franz and Charlotte can be seen, then, as embodying the same sort of foolishness which destroyed the Stock marriage. Their agony, however genuine it may be in emotional terms, is much ado about nothing. They habitually over-react, even to the slightest behavioural irregularities; and regularity, Lubitsch asserts, neither evidences nor guarantees affection. If anything, regularity tends, as the Stock marriage demonstrates, to degenerate into negative ritual, with infidelity rather than loyalty at its centre. The only real difference between the two couples is therefore one of longevity. The Franz/

Charlotte (Florence Vidor) and Gustave (Creighton Hale) in *The Marriage Circle.*

Charlotte relationship simply has not had sufficient time to go sour, but there seems little reason to doubt the probability.

Given, then, the likely course of human behaviour, and the fact that human beings necessarily exist in time (the longer things go on the worse they are likely to get), it is not surprising that the marriage circle in *The Marriage Circle* seems endless, a round-about game of error and recrimination leading ultimately to antagonism. It is certainly a cynical vision of life, although I believe it honestly represents the Ernst Lubitsch of 1925. It is nevertheless a far more profound (if stunted) vision than some critics are willing to admit. If the film is "trivial and banal,"[2] banality is not a formal flaw but the true subject of the work, a function of banal characters leading banal lives. Mizzi and Josef Stock are fascinating to a point, but only as negative examples. Their life is shallow and trivial, at least to the extent that they seem trapped in themselves and their circumstances, and *The Marriage Circle* is thus an ironic warning rather than a comic celebration. If we come away feeling a bit bewildered, it's only because Lubitsch succeeded in making his disturbing point.

* * *

The Shop Around the Corner seems, by contrast, far more good-natured and hopeful. Partly, of course, this is a function of the characters and their milieu. Matuschek & Co. — the shop around the corner — is a middle-class establishment, catering to middle-class customers, staffed by middle-class clerks and salesgirls. Unlike other Lubitsch characters, the staff members of Matuschek & Co. are busy — they have to work for a living at a time (the depression) when a living is hard to come by — and they don't have the leisure necessary to the pursuit of decadence. They have their dreams, of course, dreams of emotional and material betterment, but most of their time is spent selling leather goods and musical cigarette boxes which play "Ochi chyorniye."

But this change in milieu is indicative of a deeper, more profound change in Lubitsch's attitude toward life — and specifically in his vision of time. In *The Marriage Circle,* as we have seen, time is — given the way people use it — an essentially negative circumstance, allowing people to complicate their lives to the point of senselessness. Mizzi, in particular, comes to rely on the rituals of adultery to occupy her time, and time so occupied is at best a descending spiral, an endless cycle of pretence and betrayal. *The Shop Around the Corner* shares similar concerns — raising issues of sex and betrayal, fact and fantasy, ritual

27

and reality – but it offers more positive solutions. In other words, *The Shop Around the Corner* is concerned very deeply with the temporality of human existence and the stratagems that people may successfully employ to deal with the inevitable fact of human mortality.

It is characteristic of Lubitsch that his films "happen" at several levels, involving various and often contradictory states of awareness. So, in *The Marriage Circle,* we see Franz in his office with Mizzi. She begins to embrace him, when Gustave, Franz's partner in the medical practice, opens the door between their offices to consult with Franz. Lubitsch cuts then to a shot of Franz from the back, seen from Gustave's point of view; and all we see of Mizzi is her arms draped around Franz's shoulders. Gustave, who is secretly in love with Madame Braun, naturally assumes that Franz is embracing Charlotte: "Lucky devil, to be so loved by your own wife." Mizzi picks up the suggestion and "waves" to Gustave to complete the deception, while a rather frazzled Monte Blue smiles nervously at Gustave. Not one of these characters knows completely what is happening. Mizzi and Franz know nothing of Gustave's secret desire for Charlotte, and Gustave as yet knows nothing about Franz and Mizzi. From both perspectives life appears to be following normal routine, but we understand that routine – repeated or expected action in time – only serves here to mask more explosive, more emotionally-charged hopes and desires.

Similarly in *The Shop Around the Corner* we find that nearly everyone connected with Matuschek & Co. lives life at two levels, the level of daily activity, and the more personal, more emotional level where concepts of self-worth are formulated and fostered. Thus personal problems in nearly every case evolve from the clash of daily reality and personal fantasy. People long for meaning in their lives, and in their longing they tend to overlook the meaning that's been there all the time.

Clearly the most extreme and the most poignant example of this conflict between daily routine and emotional reality involves the boss himself, Mr. Matuschek. At first Mr. Matuschek seems very much like the Wizard of Oz (also played by Frank Morgan): tyrannical on the surface yet kindly at heart. Thus his employees fear courting his displeasure. Head clerk Alfred Kralik (James Stewart), for example, takes great pains to assure his colleague, the dapper Mr. Vadas (Joseph Schildkraut), that he intended no slight to Mrs. Matuschek's goose liver when sending Pepe (the delivery boy) for some bicarbonate of soda: "I merely said I had a little too much goose liver . . . not one word more, nor one word less"; and Pirovitch, an older clerk, always runs and hides whenever Mr. Matuschek asks for "honest" opinions. Clearly there's something to fear, otherwise the shop workers would hardly take such

28

Margaret Sullavan, Frank Morgan, and James Stewart in *The Shop Around the Corner*.

trouble to follow routine to the letter (they all arrive at work before Mr. Matuschek, as if to pass inspection) or to avoid all appearance of disharmony. But their fear could be a matter of external circumstances. As Pirovitch tells Kralik midway through the film, "millions are out of work," and the prospect of unemployment seems to be on everyone's mind.

If anything, at least in the opening scenes, Mr. Matuschek's bark seems far worse than his bite. The episode of the "Ochi chyorniye" boxes, for example, reveals Matuschek as a lovable bungler rather than a business man. Who else would spend a whole hour deciding whether he liked a poorly manufactured, imitation leather, musical cigarette box? Not a hard headed merchant, surely, but perhaps a music lover, someone who could listen to "Ochi chyorniye" twenty times a day without fatigue. Matuschek is clearly a sentimentalist at heart, less concerned with profits than with people. Thus he hired Klara Novak (Margaret Sullavan) as much for her ingenuity and her romantic frame of mind (the "Ochi chyorniye" boxes remind her of "moonlight and cigarettes and music") as for her sales ability. In fact, Matuschek & Co. is already overstaffed before Klara is hired. As we learn later, Matuschek keeps six people at work in his sparsely patronised shop, while the shop next door, twice the size, employs only four.

Yet, for all of his genuinely unself-conscious concern for his employees, Matuschek grows more and more tyrannical, even to the point of discharging Kralik and threatening to discharge Pirovitch when the latter protests against Kralik's dismissal. The generally friendly and familial routine of Matuschek & Co. is thus disrupted, and the disruption results, as we eventually discover, from the clash of practical and personal concerns. Specifically, Matuschek suspects, on the basis of an anonymous letter, that his kindness to Kralik has been betrayed. That is, Matuschek believes that Kralik has been seeing Mrs. Matuschek, and Matuschek's personal bitterness slowly infects all of his relationships, not only with Kralik, but with the rest of his employees as well.

This bitterness, however, is not a matter of cruelty or inhumanity on Matuschek's part, even if Kralik understandably perceives it as such. On the contrary, Mr. Matuschek is intensely human, as evidenced by his concern for his wife. As Mr. Matuschek puts it, after reading the private detective's dossier on Mrs. Matuschek's activities: "Twenty-two years we've been married. Twenty-two years I was proud of my wife. Well . . . she didn't want to grow old with me." And it is Matuschek's unwillingness to believe the accusation, his delay in bringing it out into the open, which allows his fear to fester into hatred. In other words, Matuschek's kind-heartedness leaves him emotionally open, completely vulnerable, and completely incapable of dealing with the situation. Like Charlotte in *The Marriage Circle*, Mr. Matuschek believed his marriage unassailable; and nothing under the sun, under the sway of time, can escape decay altogether.

Matuschek can hardly be blamed for his behaviour here; given his empathetic personality, his imperfect knowledge, and his reluctance to believe the charges, his actions are not only predictable but understandable. Nor, for that matter, can we really blame Mrs. Matuschek. We question her taste in paramours — Vadas is so patently insincere and emotionless as to call her intelligence into doubt — but she seems more to be pitied than scorned. Indeed, any woman who would desert Mr. Matuschek for an unscrupulous *gigolo* like Vadas must truly be sick at heart. The only thing Vadas has over Mr. Matuschek is youth; but the fear of mortality can drive people to extremes. In fact, it's a measure of Matuschek's extremely high regard for both his wife and Kralik that he imagines them to be lovers. Kralik, at least, is a man worth falling for, as Klara Novak eventually discovers; but it is Kralik's integrity, his worthiness of Matuschek's trust and confidence, which Matuschek ignores in his extreme anxiety. Hence Matuschek's suicide attempt when he eventually learns the truth. Not only has he been betrayed by his wife (we somehow sense he could survive that), but he has himself betrayed Kralik, by first suspecting him and then by discharging him at a time when dismissal is tantamount to ruin. Thus, whether or not we blame Mr. Matuschek for his actions, *he* certainly feels overwhelming remorse for the injustice he has done.

Comparing Mr. Matuschek to Pirovitch gives rise to one additional speculation regarding Mr. Matuschek's motives. Pirovitch (Felix Bressart) is the quintessential family man, and he keeps his family life and his work-a-day life in perspective. It is not that he is unfriendly to anyone at work; on the contrary, he is Kralik's best friend and confidant, particularly in matters having to do with marriage and Kralik's pen-pal romance. Yet it is always clear that family comes first for Pirovitch. Thus his willingness to play the "yes man" role with Mr. Matuschek. As Pirovitch puts it to Kralik: "The other day he called me an idiot. What could I do? I said, 'Yes, Mr. Matuschek, I'm an idiot.' I'm no fool." Nor is he a sycophant. His willingness to put up with Matuschek's cantankerousness reflects not only concern for his own family but empathy for Mr. Matuschek as well. Pirovitch even suggests to Kralik that Matuschek might be having "some trouble with his wife." Pirovitch is well aware that family matters can effect emotional stability.

Indeed, Pirovitch's example as a family man (he cuts down on cigars "for a few weeks" in order to afford the best physician for his ailing son) points to the fact that the Matuscheks are childless, one reason, perhaps, for Mrs. Matuschek's fear of old age. The only "child" they can be said to have is Kralik. Pirovitch understands this, and he argues against Kralik's dismissal by calling it to Matuschek's attention: "He was almost like a son to you. And you were so proud of him. You invited him to your home again and again." Kralik, indeed, was the only clerk ever invited to dine with the Matuscheks (Pepe and Vadas visited the Matuschek home only on "errands"). Hence Mr. Matuschek's suspicion. The fact that Matuschek looked upon Kralik as a son also accounts for the violence of his antipathy; in his imagination father was battling son for the sexual attentions of the mother, a classical oedipal struggle.

A similar sort of antipathy, resulting from a similar set of emotional circumstances, exists between Klara Novak and Mr. Kralik. When we first meet Miss Novak she is job-hunting, and has come to Matuschek &

31

Co. almost out of desperation ("I've got to have a job"). Kralik tries to put her off as gently as possible ("I don't know what to tell you — maybe after inventory"), but she perseveres (to Kralik's consternation) and wins Matuschek's heart by praising (and selling) his "Ochi chyorniye" boxes.

There is more to Klara than first meets the eye, however. She is, as it turns out, Kralik's pen-pal paramour, the "dear friend" in box 237, and we first become aware of her innermost longings when Kralik reads part of one of her letters to Pirovitch one morning in the relative privacy of

Lubitsch directs Pauline Frederick and May McAvoy in *Three Women.*

the stockroom. Kralik proudly points out that "she's no ordinary girl" and he offers her own words to support the contention: "We have enough troubles in our daily lives. There are so many great and beautiful things to discuss in this world of ours, it would be wasting these precious moments if we told each other the vulgar details of how we earn our daily bread."

Again we see the conflict of ordinary routine and extraordinary emotional longing. Klara and Kralik are both everyday people, both are sales clerks, yet both of them long for something better. Their longings, however, carry implications of self-disgust (of the sort that drive Mr. Matuschek to suicide). Klara's attack on Kralik ("I really wouldn't care to scratch your surface, Mr. Kralik, because I know exactly what I'd find: instead of a heart, a handbag, instead of a soul, a suitcase, instead of an intellect, a cigarette lighter, which doesn't work") is equally, therefore, an attack on herself. Like Mrs. Matuschek, Klara and Kralik are dissatisfied with life as it is, and they ask more out of life than life can deliver. Hence they fear disappointment, and in their fear they are unwilling to grant others the depth of emotion which they assume for themselves.

Klara thus sees herself leading a double life. There is the stultifying, meaningless life of her everyday salesgirl routine, a life of handbags, suitcases, and cigarette lighters; and her place in that routine carries no privilege: she is simply another salesgirl like all the other salesgirls. And then there is her life as a "modern girl," a life of feeling, of culture, of privileged knowledge and privileged moments. Klara sees herself, therefore, as something special, essentially unlike her middle-class peers. Therein lies her mistake. She naturally assumes, her own example notwithstanding, that clerks cannot be genuinely interesting or attractive or human. Thus when the right clerk comes along she almost loses him. To be sure, she does not ignore Kralik altogether. In fact, her animosity towards him results not from disinterest but attraction, as she confesses to Kralik in the film's closing moments: "I just couldn't take my eyes off of you . . . and all the time I kept saying to myself, 'Klara Novak, what on earth is the matter with you? This Kralik is not a particularly attractive type of man.' " Put another way, Klara becomes angry with Kralik for letting her fall in love with him, and the last thing she wants to do is fall in love with a clerk. Kralik, therefore, finds himself involved in two fantastic and illusory love triangles. On the one hand he is suspected of romancing Mrs. Matuschek; and on the other he threatens Klara's image of the perfect love affair. That is, Kralik the clerk competes with Kralik the cultured pen-pal for the attentions of Miss Novak — who is not quite sure who she is.

Kralik also longs for a better life, though in his case the longing does not require complete rejection of his everyday self. He merely wishes to broaden his horizons. As he puts it to Pirovitch: "You come to a time in your life when you get tired of going to cafés, dance halls, every night. You want to improve yourself. For example, you want to study something about art, literature, and history, how people live in Brazil." His search for broader knowledge leads him to the Sunday paper, where he turns to the wrong page and comes across Klara's pen-pal ad. He is attracted by her desire to correspond on "cultural subjects," and their postal courtship begins. Before long, however, the focus of Kralik's attention shifts from questions of culture to the question of marriage, and he begins to consult Pirovitch on the practical realities of married life, how much it costs to live, and so on.

Two factors stand in the way of this comic movement toward marriage: Kralik's financial situation (he feels he must get a rise before getting married) and his fear of disappointing or being disappointed (he does not want to spoil the dream by facing reality). Indeed, his plea of poverty may only be an excuse to postpone meeting his pen-pal. As he expresses it (again to Pirovitch): "Did you ever get a bonus? . . . When the boss hands you the envelope you wonder how much is in it. You don't want to open it. As long as the envelope's closed you're a millionaire." It is this delay, more than anything else, which threatens the Klara/Kralik relationship. The longer Kralik postpones meeting his "dear friend," the more intense becomes the animosity between Kralik the clerk and Klara the salesgirl. Indeed, their mutual animosity is so great by the time Kralik approaches Klara in the cafe that he dares not reveal his pen-pal identity. It took time (six months, to be exact) for their mutual antagonism to develop, and it will take time to defuse the situation.

Herein lies the difference between *The Marriage Circle* and *The Shop Around the Corner.* In the former film time is a negative circumstance, for it allows people to compound their foolishness past the point of no return. In *The Shop Around the Corner,* on the other hand, time is both a threat (to Mrs. Matuschek, for example), and an opportunity. Thus Mr. Matuschek may let time so confound his emotions that he attempts suicide, but time also allows circumstance for his recovery. Similarly, time allows Klara and Kralik to build up fantastic dreams and equally intense anxieties, but it also allows the opportunity to go beyond anxiety to something more rewarding.

Time, therefore, is both a harrowing and a healing circumstance. Structurally speaking, *The Shop Around the Corner* is a progression in time through stages of darkness, disappointment, and agony to a final stage of promise and renewal. The film begins in early June — Matuschek & Co. is having its summer sale — and it is in June that Klara joins the staff and that Kralik dines with the Matuscheks. But already there are premonitions of the problems to come. Vadas is already dapper beyond his means. Mr. Matuschek is in a proverbial bad mood, as Kralik tells Klara. Indeed, Matuschek is already concerned about the relationship between Kralik and Mrs. Matuschek. His tentative, questioning tone of voice when he tells Kralik that "Mrs. Matuschek thinks a lot of you, and I think a lot of Mrs. Matuschek" indicates some measure of fear or suspicion even at this early point in the film.

The film's second day takes place in winter, in early December. The air is cold, the streets are full of snow, and Mr. Matuschek's suspicions have progressed to the point of hiring a private detective (as did Professor Stock in *The Marriage Circle*) to investigate his wife's activities. By now Vadas is taking a taxi to work and flashing a big roll of bills, while Klara and Kralik have reached a double accord: as fellow

"Dear friends": Kralik (James Stewart) and Miss Novak (Margaret Sullavan).

clerks they have agreed to hate each other (for example, their argument over her blouse and his tie), and as pen-pal lovers they have finally agreed to meet. The day is, therefore, fraught with anxiety for nearly everyone in the shop. Matuschek fears what he may learn from the detective. Klara and Kralik anxiously anticipate their evening rendez-vous (as pen-pals they are to meet for the first time), and their hopes give rise to new fears when Mr. Matuschek insists that everyone work late to change the window displays. Not only must they both master their fear of meeting "dear friend," but now they must risk Matuschek's displeasure by asking for the night off.

The worst happens in nearly every case. Not only does Matuschek learn that his wife has deserted him, but he learns he has wrongly suspected and dismissed Kralik as well. Not only does Kralik not get a rise, but he is fired outright. And Klara not only suffers the embarrassment of being stood up (or so it seems to her), but in her disappointment she is forced to put up with Kralik's unwelcome attentions. Indeed, the reality of this day is far worse than anyone's worst fantasy. But in coming to terms with this reality both Matuschek and Kralik are able to shed misconceptions and to move on to more genuinely fruitful, more legitimately realistic, modes of thought and behaviour.

Dawn of the film's third day thus begins the upward emotional swing. Kralik visits Mr. Matuschek in the hospital, they are reconciled, and Matuschek appoints Kralik manager of Matuschek & Co. Indeed, the transfer of power takes on religious overtones as Matuschek hands over the keys to his middle-class kingdom, and the religiosity is reinforced when Kralik promises that "this will be the biggest Christmas in the history of Matuschek & Co." Kralik then returns to the store, where he is greeted by his joyful fellow workers. Even Vadas, sensing which way the wind now blows, tries to get into the act, hypocritically welcoming Kralik back to the shop. But Kralik, at Mr. Matuschek's urging, dismisses Vadas. Vadas thus serves the scapegoat role; he is acquisitiveness carried to the extreme, and represents the worst of middle-class qualities. His dismissal, therefore, takes on symbolic overtones, as if Kralik were banishing not only a second-class clerk but a genuinely evil spirit. Klara then enters, very distraught ("I can hardly see straight"), asking for Mr. Matuschek. Kralik tries to tell her that he is now the store manager, and she refuses to believe him: he is still a clerk in her eyes. Only when a phone call confirms Kralik's promotion does Klara acknowledge the fact — by fainting.

The third day thus ends where it began, with Kralik visiting another sick-bed, except now it is Klara who has suffered the emotional breakdown. Her collapse differs from Mr. Matuschek's in that it does not result from discovering the truth. She still believes that Kralik exists on another planet, and she remains distraught at being abandoned by her pen-pal. Furthermore, Klara rather enjoys the melancholia of it all: at least she has something in common with Emma Bovary. Kralik's task, then, and the purpose of his visit, is to bring her out of her trance, to get her back to the shop, and finally to make her see the truth. Thus he writes another "dear friend" letter, explaining his absence at the café, as a means of getting her back on her emotional feet, ready to face the real world again. She still sees her dream lover and Kralik as complete opposites ("where you would say 'black,' he would say 'white' "), but she eventually comes to admire the rhetoric with which he praises wallets as "quite romantic." As she exclaims: "Why Mr. Kralik, you

"Klara, darling. . . ."

surprise me, that's very well expressed." Kralik's metaphor remains middle-class, to be sure, but wallets can carry love letters and snapshots as well as money; and Klara begins to see that Kralik's suitcase soul carries genuine concern rather than stuffed shirts — a step in the right direction.

The film's fourth and final day is December 24. Klara is back at work, looking forward to a Christmas Eve meeting with her pen-pal, and before the shop closes its doors Mr. Matuschek is also back on his feet and back on the floor of Matuschek & Co. He could not stay away from his family on Christmas Eve ("this is my home; this is where I spent most of my life") and he distributes Christmas bonuses as a means of apologising to those he had hurt and of expressing his gratitude to those who stood by him. Then they all go their separate ways, Pirovitch home to his family, Pepe to his girl friend, Mr. Matuschek and Rudy, the new delivery boy, go off together for a Christmas dinner of roast goose with all the trimmings — leaving only Klara and Kralik alone in the locker room. Moved by the conciliatory spirit of Christmas, Klara confesses to being attracted to Kralik; and Kralik proceeds to disillusion her, first by destroying her image of "dear friend," who is, according to Kralik, a bald-headed, paunchy, out-of-work, money-grubbing fellow named Popkin, and then by revealing his own identity: "Klara, darling . . . please take your key and open post office box 237 and take me out of my envelope and kiss me." They do kiss, but only after Kralik raises his trousers to prove he is not bow-legged.

The Shop Around the Corner, then, is concerned to raise the trousers, as it were, to look beyond the surface of middle-class life to the emotional reality beneath. Even clerks can feel very deeply the need for love and understanding. Their lives can be rich and dangerous and eventful, even to the point of suicide; but no matter how bad things get, no matter what the magnitude of emotional catastrophe, there is always the chance of renewal and regeneration. If Christ can be born, be crucified, and be reborn, so too can Mr. Matuschek pick up the pieces of his life and start anew, so too can Klara and Kralik find a way to love without fear of being ordinary.

The Shop Around the Corner is both thematically and stylistically an intensely humane film, as is memorably evidenced in its closing moments. It centres attention on people and their problems with little extraneous or self-conscious cinematic flash. As Richard Corliss says, "the famed Lubitsch touch is here more of a caress."[3] *The Shop Around the Corner* is an acted film, a spoken film, photographed for the most part in eloquently simple two-shot, which allows Lubitsch to focus on interaction and emotion. There are moments of ingenuity —

James Stewart and Donna Reed in Frank Capra's *It's a Wonderful Life.*

the shots of Pirovitch's feet running up the stairs, the quick tracking shot of Kralik as he marches in hopeful anticipation to Mr. Matuschek's office, the shot of Klara's gloved hand forlornly searching her empty post office box — but even these moments serve primarily to reinforce the emotional reality created by dramatic situations. Those situations can be terrifying in their implications, yet it is the measure of Lubitsch's humanism, his belief in the significance of life and its possibilities, that he never lets terror overcome hope. *The Shop Around the Corner* belongs, therefore, with that handful of Hollywood films — *City Lights, Only Angels Have Wings, How Green Was My Valley, It's a*

39

Wonderful Life — in which full emotional intensity and absolute conceptual clarity are perfectly aligned. We have here no cycle of despair (although despair is clearly accounted for) but a legitimate vision of love and hope transcending time; no greater gift exists.

2 Frivolity and Responsibility: *Lady Windermere's Fan* (1925), *The Student Prince* (1927), and *The Merry Widow* (1934)

Lady Windermere's Fan, next to *The Marriage Circle* Lubitsch's best-known silent film, is concerned with social reality and social illusion; the reality in this case being a strong set of social rules, and the illusion being that one can break those rules with impunity. To be sure, it is always possible in Lubitsch to break with upper-crust society altogether, as happens in *Design for Living* and *Trouble in Paradise.* But in both of these films the central characters never really "belonged" in society to begin with. They are outsiders who enter society, either on false pretences (Lily and Gaston in *Trouble*) or out of a sort of social-climbing curiosity (Tom, George, and Gilda in *Design*). They have, therefore, no great emotional stake in maintaining their place in the world of high society. Indeed, their emotions tend either to transcend class (Gaston genuinely cares for Madame Colet) or to reject class in the service of less conventional but no less genuine relationships (the *menage à trois* which concludes *Design*).

In *Lady Windermere's Fan,* however, class counts, counts for just about everything, so that one's place in the social order is a matter of no small significance. Indeed, the film begins with the issue of place: "Lady Windermere was facing the grave problem — of seating her dinner guests." Specifically, where should Lord Darlington (Ronald Colman) be seated, and, perhaps more importantly, where does Lady Windermere (May McAvoy) want him to sit, next to her, or elsewhere?

41

Gary Cooper, Miriam Hopkins, and Fredric March in *Design for Living.*

Lady Windermere is clearly uncertain of herself, and her hand (in close-up) hesitates as she places Lord Darlington's card next to her own place in her wooden mock-up of the dinner table. She is clearly toying with the notion of flirtation here, as if it were a harmless and inconsequential game of some sort, and she is encouraged in this regard by her social position. People of her class are professional game players: it's a way of life. People go calling, to the races at Royal Ascot, to elegant parties, they go for walks in the garden, they go shopping for expensive birthday presents (ivory fans, for example) — but not one goes to work. If Lady Berwick (Carrie d'Aumery) and her school for scandal work at anything, they work at watching how well others play the social game.

There is a tendency, then, as evidenced by Lady Windermere's behaviour, to let playfulness get out of hand. Of course, she thinks she has good reason, believing quite mistakenly that her husband is cheating on her, but she carries things too far, to the point of deserting Lord Windermere (Bert Lytell) in favour of Lord Darlington. To be sure, Darlington is a fine enough fellow, very much like her husband in fact (the similarity between Darlington and Lord Windermere anticipates that of the Herbert Marshall/Melvyn Douglas characters in *Angel*).[4] Darlington's only fault, after all, is telling what he believes to be the truth, that Lord Windermere is providing Mrs. Erlynne (who is, it turns out, Lady Windermere's mother) with financial support. Darlington's

Lady Windermere's Fan: Lady Windermere (May McAvoy) clings to her husband (Bert Lytell) as Lord Darlington (Ronald Colman) looks on.

An *Angel's* dilemma: Lady Barker (Marlene Dietrich) caught between her husband, Sir Frederick (Herbert Marshall), and her lover, Anthony Halton (Melvyn Douglas).

motive, furthermore, is love, and there is no reason to doubt his sincerity. Indeed, he proves his sincerity when he decides to leave England. He clearly loves Lady Windermere so much that he will sacrifice his own happiness to insure her emotional welfare. He knows that his continued presence will only mean heartbreak for both of them.

The likelihood of that heartbreak is demonstrated by Mrs. Erlynne (Irene Rich), Lady Windermere's mother, who knows full well what it means to break the rules of the social game. She had once done so, leaving her husband and daughter behind for the sake of an earlier Lord Darlington, and she has had to pay the price. She will always remain a stranger to her daughter (who believes her mother to be dead), and she has had to survive as an adventuress, drifting from one liaison to the next. Hence her anxiety: she is ageing (the ever-vigilant Lady Berwick spots a gray hair) and her days as an adventuress are numbered. She is well aware of upper-class hypocrisy, but she values upper-class amenities. In other words, Mrs. Erlynne longs for the security that Lord Lorton (Edward Martindel), London's most eligible bachelor, represents, and she sets out to win his attention and affections (hence her trip to the race track). She wants to re-enter society, and she must make her move before she becomes another Lady Berwick, all bark and no beauty. She therefore "blackmails" Lord Windermere, threatening to reveal her true identity, and he reluctantly agrees to finance her charade. He cannot buy back her lost reputation, but he can, and to his credit he does, provide the wherewithal necessary for her assault on society.

But it's not a matter of gold-digging on Mrs. Erlynne's part, of pretending to be something she is not. She had a reputation to lose, after all, and her experience has clearly given her a strong sense of self-worth. Indeed, the famous race track sequence is doubly significant. To begin with, of course, Royal Ascot allowed Lubitsch a marvellous opportunity for social satire. The upper crust is out in force, with all of the pomp and ceremony (including bagpipers) appropriate to genteel sport — the women all dressed to the teeth, the men all tailed and top-hatted. Furthermore, Lubitsch shot the scene on location, out of doors, away from the artificial confines of too-perfect drawing rooms and too-formal gardens; thus it is all the more striking that artificiality should still be the order of the day. Life at the track is all ritual, circularity, moving fast but going nowhere. Indeed, while everyone else watches the race, Lady Berwick and her crew watch Mrs. Erlynne; and they can do so because the race doesn't really matter.

It is therefore appropriate that critics should focus on the satiric aspects of the scene. People actually treat Mrs. Erlynne like a prize filly, training their field-glasses on her as if she were running in the next race. But something else happens at the same time; for not only do we see people gawking, but we see much more clearly what they are gawking at. At first Lubitsch cuts between objective shots of the gawkers, and subjective shots of Mrs. Erlynne as seen from the gawker point of view, using masks over the camera lens to frame Mrs. Erlynne in the overlapping circles which signify binocular vision. Mrs. Erlynne is thus isolated from her surroundings. We see her for herself, a woman of elegance and self-possession. Eventually we lose a sense of the immediate social milieu as Lubitsch drops the objective shots altogether. Instead, we get a marvellous dissolve montage of Mrs. Erlynne seen from a variety of angles. We see her every facet, and from every perspective she is an extraordinary woman, beautiful, mature, high-spirited. In other words, she stands out in the crowd, and in our imagination, for very good reason. We must keep in mind, however, that Mrs. Erlynne's *savoir faire,* and hence our admiration of her, cannot be separated from the fact of her original class standing. She is no Liza Doolittle, and her sense of self is inextricably bound up with her class background. Put another way, we cannot admire her without accepting, as she accepts, the fact of society's rules, which can in no real sense be changed. The best she can hope to accomplish is to loosen society up a bit, enough at least, to allow her re-entrance. Perhaps society will be the better for her presence, a little slower to jump to erroneous conclusions, but it is doubtful.

Mrs. Erlynne's dilemma, then, has to do with the conflict between concern for herself and concern for her daughter. Both concerns are one in that Lady Windermere threatens to repeat her mother's original mistake. Mrs. Erlynne, who knows how such mistakes are made, and what comes of making them, must choose; either to re-enact her fallen-woman role by walking into a room full of men at Lord Darlington's suite and accepting responsibility for the fan that Lady Windermere left so conspicuously on the couch, knowing full well that to do so in Lord Lorton's presence risks alienating him for good; or to let her daughter take the blame.

Knowing her as we do, we do not doubt that Mrs. Erlynne will make the right, the moral, choice. She can make that choice because she understands the social terms in which upper-class people think. She knows how quickly people are likely to make rush judgements, no matter how questionable the evidence. Indeed, the film can be understood as a long series of false estimations. Lord Windermere assumes that Mrs. Erlynne is a common blackmailer, and is taken aback to discover that she is his mother-in-law. Similarly, at film's end, and despite his experience in the first instance, Lord Windermere persists in snubbing Mrs. Erlynne as a whore: he saw her at Lord Darlington's and that is evidence enough in his eyes. Lord Darlington likewise jumps to the conclusion that Lord Windermere keeps Mrs. Erlynne as a mistress. Almost everyone at the racetrack assumes that Mrs. Erlynne is a gold-digger. Lord Lorton assumes on two different occasions that Mrs. Erlynne is a shameless woman (the first instance, in which Lorton takes his own cigar butt as evidence of infidelity, foreshadows the second incident, with the fan). Also, Lady Windermere, like Darlington, believes that her husband has something going with Mrs. Erlynne. The only person with sufficient scepticism and self-awareness to avoid such perceptual/conceptual mistakes is Mrs. Erlynne herself, and our sympathy with her results partly from the fact that we see things from

Mothers and daughters: Pauline Frederick and May McAvoy (above) in *Three Women* and Irene Rich and May McAvoy (below) in *Lady Windermere's Fan.*

Lady Windermere and Lord Darlington confront the situation.

her point of view. Lubitsch, like Hitchcock, very seldom fools us; instead he lets us watch others being fooled. So, for example, when Lady Windermere sees someone kissing Mrs. Erlynne's hand on the porch during the party scene, she naturally assumes it is her husband who is doing the kissing, despite the fact that the gentleman is blocked from her view by an ivy-covered column. But the thought never enters our mind, except as we recognise it in hers. We know both Mrs. Erlynne and Lord Windermere too well to make such an ill-timed inductive leap, and, as it turns out, we are right: it was Lord Lorton all the while.

The film has, therefore, a double point. First of all, Lubitsch argues, people should be sceptical, they should not jump to false conclusions, particularly in regard to other people's motives or morals. As the film demonstrates, however, few characters are capable of maintaining such a properly sceptical stance. To do so would take much of the scandal and much of the fun out of an otherwise frivolous though comfortable existence. Accepting this tendency for false estimation as a social fact, then, Lubitsch (via Mrs. Erlynne) counsels, as his second point, social caution. If people are likely to misinterpret the slightest irregularity of behaviour, then people had better take care to maintain an adequate degree of self-control. Such control is not to be completely equated with selfishness or banality. It is Mrs. Erlynne's self-control and social acumen which allows her to save her daughter. She knows the sort of conclusions people are likely to jump to, and she plays to those expectations when she claims the fan at Lord Darlington's. It is, of course, highly improbable that she could absent-mindedly walk off with such an ornate fan, particularly when she does not carry a fan herself; but probability carries little weight in a Wildean world of surfaces and superficiality. Furthermore, it is self-control, of an admittedly outland-ish sort, that allows Mrs. Erlynne to regain Lord Lorton's attentions. They meet, quite by chance, as she is leaving the Windermere mansion for the last time, having said farewell to her daughter. As they stop for a moment, Mrs. Erlynne seizes the Wildean initiative, turning the tables on her disappointed suitor by berating him for *his* behaviour: "Your conduct last night was outrageous. I have decided not to marry you." Lorton is, as we are, appropriately impressed by her style and he joins her in the taxi.

It would be a mistake, I believe, to read this ending as implying any measure of social change. Lorton, after all, is rather daring for his age and station, and it is not a complete surprise when he tosses propriety over for Mrs. Erlynne's sake; after all, he can afford it. If anything, we should count the reconciliation as an ironic epilogue, a privileged moment in which Lubitsch allows himself the pleasure of rewarding his leading lady with an attenuated sort of social acceptance. She is now Lady Lorton. Their marriage, however, is still somewhat mercenary, and the only real "lovers" in the film, Lord and Lady Windermere, remain at odds over Mrs. Erlynne's virtue (Lord Lorton leaves the room rather than wish her farewell). Thus the plot is resolved, but the issue of social cruelty resists solution.

* * *

The Student Prince, at first viewing, seems far less caustic, far more pastoral, and far less Lubitsch than *Lady Windermere's Fan.* Much of it is set in the country, the boisterous university town of Old Heidelberg, and the central character is not a worldly wise adventuress but an innocently wide-eyed crown prince (Ramon Novarro), who tastes, for

At hazard in society: Pola Negri as *Madame DuBarry* (above) and Irene Rich as Mrs. Erlynne (below).

the first time, the normal joys of youth. Yet, despite these obvious dissimilarities, both films deal with like issues — class duty vs. emotional integrity, innocence vs. experience — and in both cases the imperatives of class require the sacrifice of the ideal to the real. If anything, *The Student Prince* comes off as the more melancholy film, because Karl Heinrich, the student prince, cannot avoid his royal destiny. He literally becomes a class unto himself — becomes King Karl — and the film is a lyrical meditation upon the price that Karl must pay for privilege.

In structure the film recalls *The Marriage Circle*. A world of social experience, in this case the world of courtly pomp and circumstance, brackets and threatens to destroy a world of innocent sexuality. The contrast is clearer, of course, in *The Student Prince:* the court and Heidelberg are far removed from each other, so far removed that Karl-the-student fits readily into the fellowship of Saxonians (a privilege gained, not by birth, but by capacity for drink — Karl must drain his *stein* at one pull); and furthermore, the film's sexuality, as embodied in the Karl/Kathi (Norma Shearer) relationship, is child-like without being childish. Novarro's Karl Heinrich is a genuine romantic, and his sudden passion for Kathi, though conventional to the degree that it is love at first sight, is never coy or insincere. And we can surely understand his feelings for Kathi; as played by Norma Shearer, and photographed by Lubitsch and cameraman John Mescall, Kathi is a completely believable incarnation of the Pre-Raphaelite damsel. Indeed, her flowing clothes, her wavy hair, her long elegant neck, are the very stuff of adolescent fantasy. But it is a fantasy made real to us, and to Karl, by Lubtisch's eloquent use of extreme close-up. It's an unusual visual tactic for Lubitsch, but like Griffith in *Broken Blossoms* or Borzage in *Seventh Heaven,* Lubitsch uses it in *The Student Prince* to intensify and legitimise our sense of Kathi's reality. We get as close to her as cameras could then get, and she withstands our gaze. It's not a matter of seeing through her to discover questionable motives — as is the case with Charlotte in *The Marriage Circle* — but of seeing her truly, as she lives and breathes, a woman without guile or gullibility.

The first section of *The Student Prince* sets out the essential issues. "In the Kingdom of Karlsburg there was great excitement — the people were to see for their first time the crown prince," — and the crown prince, in turn, is to see for the first time not only the people but the sort of behaviour expected of those in positions of public trust. Of course, Lubitsch treats the pomp and circumstance of the Prince's arrival in an appropriately satiric style. The public show of reverence for the royal family is a bit mechanical (everyone taking off their top hats in unison, for example) but the society needs, or so the film implies, its

The Student Prince (Ramon Novarro) rides high in Heidelberg.

reverential symbols and ceremonies. Indeed, the people themselves make the point clear: they drink enthusiastically to the king's portrait, and they gather excitedly to see the latest photograph of the prince. The images are deceptive in both cases. The king seems far sterner in person than his portrait would seem to indicate (Lubitsch makes this clear by dissolving from portrait to king); and the prince, similarly, seems far happier, as a child amidst his many toys, or far more debonair, as a dashing, well-tailored dandy, than is ever the case in actual fact.

This distance between emotional fact and public image is specified when the prince, as a sailor-suited youngster, steps off the train to meet his uncle, the king. Everyone but the king bows, cannons roar in salute, and the boy, panic-stricken, quickly retreats into his railroad car. The king is clearly displeased. He sneers beneath his moustache, taps his foot impatiently, and waits while the boy's nurse pushes the reluctant prince forward. Whether he wants to or not, the lad must disregard his own feelings, in this instance his understandable fear, not only of the cannons, but of his stern-faced uncle, and carry through his ceremonial duties, shaking hands, riding in parade through the streets, and so on.

Appearance thus overrides the reality of feeling. The prince is trapped in his role, trapped without playmates within the confines of the royal estate, and his only positive relationship, once the king sends the boy's nurse away, is with his tutor, Dr. Juttner (Jean Hersholt). Juttner's mission, as the king describes it, is to instruct the prince in "etiquette, obligation, duty, demeanor, and formality," that is, in the arts of public duty and public ceremony. Juttner, to his credit, disregards the king's charge, and he seems far more concerned to instruct the boy in the arts of self-realisation, playing soccer, wrestling, pillow fighting and sneaking a smoke. Thus it is an appropriate and necessary step in Juttner's effort to humanely educate the prince that he secure the king's consent to send Karl Heinrich to the university at Heidelberg.

The journey to Heidelberg is, for the prince, a passage from darkness to light, from bondage to freedom, from solemnity to frivolity.[5] Heidelberg and its people are characterised by a precise lack of the sort of artifice that typifies the king and his courtiers. There is ceremony, of course, but the country ceremonials require little if any distance between feeling and form. Thus when the Saxonians raise their beer steins in unison, it is expressive of their genuine and joyful sense of community, of shared experience. Indeed, Kathi greets the prince upon his arrival, not with cannons, but with flowers, and the ceremony, though marked by Kathi's inability to remember her lines (her forgetfulness prompted by her personal interest in the prince), celebrates the expression of feeling rather than its suppression.

Kathi herself embodies the natural sympathy of person and place. She is a country girl, a spring princess ("these fairest flowers of spring, to you, Oh Prince, a message bring") and she clearly feels none of Karl Heinrich's discomfort. Her role and her feelings are perfectly in tune: hence Karl Heinrich's interest. Not only is she a beautiful girl, but she fascinates by virtue of her emotional and sexual integrity. Her sexuality, indeed, is overt though always charming (she quite unselfconsciously shows the prince how sturdy and comfortable his bed is) and she clearly enjoys the attentions of the Saxonians (they carry her enthusiastically around on their shoulders after she drains a stein of beer at their prompting). Karl is understandably drawn to her — she treats him as an equal ("the prince, after all, is only a human being") —

and their courtship is as delicate and charming as anything in Griffith or Borzage. Time seems to stop, and for a moment tenderness transcends the facts of birth and station.

But the film makes it clear that such tenderness, however real and vital, cannot last. The king's health, even before Karl Heinrich departs from Karlsburg, is failing; once in Heidelberg, Karl's liveried servant constantly intrudes as a reminder of Karl's position; Dr. Juttner then

The Student Prince: Ramon Novarro as Prince Karl Heinrich and Norma Shearer as his Heidelberg sweetheart.

receives a dispatch announcing the king's decision that Karl shall marry a royal princess of the king's choosing (Juttner hasn't the heart to tell the prince); and the fearfully expected eventually happens — Karl is called back to court to assume the royal duties during his uncle's illness. The prince agrees to leave Heidelberg, on the hope of returning when the king recovers, and the prince and Kathi slowly, reluctantly pack his belongings, his student cap, his Saxonian ribbons, his photograph of Kathi, both sensing, rightly, that Karl will never return, that they will never recapture their now lost innocence.

Their premonitions prove accurate. Winter overtakes Spring, rain replaces sunshine, the king dies, more human in death than in life, the kindly Dr. Juttner dies as well, and Karl is completely on his own, carrying the full responsibility of government upon his sorrow-bent shoulders. But he carries the burden with great reluctance. He keeps his Heidelberg mementoes in his royal desk, and his mind wanders in daydream back to Kathi and Heidelberg, imagining the reception he will get at his return (carried on the shoulders of the Saxonians) and the expression on Kathi's face when she sees her prince again. Karl suffers here from an adolescent sort of emotionalism (something like Paul's war-induced hysteria in *The Man I Killed*), and Lubitsch emphasises the

The Saxonian toast: cold and ritualistic.

force of Karl's preoccupation by zooming in and out of the day-dream sequence. Dreams, however, count for little in the film, and fantasy notwithstanding, Karl is made to recognise, however slowly, however painfully, the force of circumstance. Thus he reluctantly signs the royal order for his marriage to Princess Ilse, and even his sudden decision to return to Heidelberg is couched in terms of his impending wedding. Karl strides across his enormous royal office, and raises a toast to Dr. Juttner's portrait: "Just one more day of life, Doctor – one day of life – and love."

Phillips Holmes plays a "broken lullaby" in *The Man I Killed*.

Unhappily, the Heidelberg that Karl had known is no longer. The garden has become a graveyard, leaf strewn, autumnal, devoid of laughter and fellowship. The seasons have changed and Karl has changed with them. He is now King Karl, and that fact alone eliminates all chance of reliving or retrieving past pleasure. Thus when the

Saxonians gather to toast Karl, they do so in full military regalia (Karl is their commander-in-chief), and their toast, however sincerely meant, is stiffly ritualistic. Their respect for Karl has not diminished, their filing-out *en masse* while Karl and Kathi embrace is genuinely touching in its empathetic regard for the couple's privacy, but their kindest gesture still has the effect of isolating the prince. All he has left is Kathi, and, as she makes clear in the following exchange, all he will eventually be able to retain is the memory of their Heidelberg summer. As Kathi puts it: "You see, Karl Heinrich, it never could have been any different."

The Student Prince, then, is a touching, eloquent parable of failure, of humankind's inevitable failure to overcome the fact of time. Like *The Man I Killed,* which it precedes and closely resembles, *The Student Prince* is "a terrifying poem of love and death."[6] Both films move from the city (Karlsberg or Paris) to the country; in each instance the adolescent hero seeks happiness – or at least pretends to it – and each boy eventually falls in love; in both cases death comes between the lovers, the death of Karl's uncle, the death, at Paul's hands, of Elsa's soldier *fiancé* (the man Paul killed); and in both films the hero must adopt a difficult social role, not for his own sake, but for the sake of those who depend upon him. Indeed, the hero in both films is last seen in similarly ironic close-ups, Karl Heinrich riding joylessly in the marriage procession through the streets of Karlsberg, Paul Renard (Phillips Holmes) playing a violin which once belonged to the man he killed. Karl thus replaces his dead uncle; and Paul replaces the Holderin's dead son. But in neither case do we sense resolution. We rather sense a bitter-sweet regret that life could not be otherwise. As Elsa (Nancy Carroll) tells Paul in *The Man I Killed:* "You're not going to kill Walter a second time. You're going to live, for them .... I don't matter, and neither do you. It's them we have to think of."[7]

* * *

Both *Lady Windermere's Fan* and *The Student Prince* reflect upon the conflict of social necessity and personal well-being. In the earlier film Mrs. Erlynne attains the fortune she had been hunting as reward for properly motivated action. That is, she achieves a desired social status only because she willingly risked that status in the service of her daughter's happiness. In *The Student Prince,* on the other hand, personal and social demands are clearly at odds: the king's death requires the prince to carry the burden of social responsibility at the expense of emotional integrity. *The Merry Widow* raises similar issues, beginning where *The Student Prince* ends, at a point where social and

Romantic myth: Dietrich and Cooper in Frank Borzage's *Desire*, produced by Ernst Lubitsch.

personal imperatives conflict, and it concludes at a point where distinctions between personal and social imperatives collapse. In other words, *The Merry Widow* carries beyond the social realism of *Lady Windermere's Fan* into the emotionally charged realm of romantic myth.

Both *The Student Prince* and *The Merry Widow* have death as a central fact; and while the death in *The Merry Widow* takes place before the story commences, it colours the opening sequence. The widow Sonia (Jeannette MacDonald) is a spectral presence, always dressed in mourning black, her face forever veiled from public view.

Like the student prince, Sonia, by virtue of her position, bears a great measure of social responsibility. She owns over fifty per cent of the kingdom, as the hapless King Achmed II (George Barbier) tells his over-curious queen (she's always asking when he'll return from cabinet meetings: she has to arrange her amatory schedule), and Sonia's presence in the kingdom is all that keeps the royal Marshovian treasury afloat. Should she marry and leave the kingdom the king will be flat on his throne. Her continued presence in Marshovia, however, only reinforces her sense of isolation (e.g. her diary nearly full of blank pages). Like many an upper-class lady in Lubitsch, she stays at home, doing nothing: but Sonia hasn't even a husband to cheat on. Instead she walks the streets at night, eavesdropping on gypsy fiddlers; or she sings from her castle balcony. Indeed, until her departure for Paris, Sonia's only social act is her song: she sings, the fiddler plays, and Chevalier conducts as his orderly croons a romantic reply.

The very fact of her singing, however, indicates that things are about to change, to Sonia's elation and the kingdom's distress. Her meeting with Captain Danilo (Chevalier), and his outrageously self-confident assault on her privacy, calls that privacy into question. As she tells him that evening, she'd leave mourning "in a minute if there were any reason for it," and Danilo, whether Sonia admits it to herself or not, provides all the reason she needs. It is immediately after the meeting with Danilo that she sings her song of longing, standing on her balcony in a low-cut, off-the-shoulder, though still black, *negligée*. Thus, while she remains technically in mourning, her thoughts, as her diary subsequently reveals, have turned to less solemn pursuits. Indeed, Danilo has effectively reawakened her dormant sexuality (recall the splendidly frivolous lingerie she slips into), and she decides to leave for Paris immediately. Her departure, however, throws Achmed and his court into a crisis. Reports from Paris indicate that Sonia is beleaguered by fortune-hunting suitors, and the King sends his most qualified man, Captain Danilo (qualified by virtue of his liaison with the queen) as a special envoy. Like the student prince, Danilo must swallow his integrity and marry a woman of the king's choosing. Otherwise the king will have to pack up his crown and call it a day.

Fortunately for Danilo, and for us as well, the conflict between personal and social responsibilities is more apparent than real. As it turns out, Sonia and Danilo are made for each other. Their repartee, in the opening encounter, sparkles with one-upmanship (*Danilo:* "Are you pretty . . . or beautiful?" *Sonia:* "Gorgeous."), and their dance numbers, particularly at the embassy ball, are exquisitely timed and coordinated. Indeed, Lubitsch involves us directly in their dance of love. For example, in their first dance number, which takes place in

Danilo's private "dining room" at Maxim's, Sonia and Danilo glide effortlessly, elegantly, sensually around the room, and the camera just as effortlessly follows their every movement.

This lack of effort accounts, I believe, for the generally positive tone of the film. Danilo is openly enthusiastic about life, Sonia, once in Paris, is equally as alive (recall how quickly she gets into the spirit of things at Maxim's: "I'm just in the mood for a banker"); and the social issue (the rise and fall of Marshovia) takes second place to the personal: will Sonia and Danilo disentangle their confused relationship before confusion deepens to complete distrust? Hence Lubitsch's generally light-hearted treatment of Marshovian politics. King Achmed and his crew, including Edward Everett Horton's marvellously inept Count Popov, the ambassador to France, are a bunch of lovable bunglers, self-important without really being self-indulgent. We do not take them very seriously, and Lubitsch clearly had no intention that they be taken as anything other than marvellous musical-comedy buffoons. As the Chamberlain puts it to Achmed: "They are even telling jokes about your majesty." The King's reply ("Are they funny?") indicates his properly comic place in the scheme of things.

The one thing that we do take seriously is the Sonia/Danilo relationship, which recalls, in its moments of tenderness, and in the visual treatment Lubitsch accords it (the exquisite close-ups of Jeanette MacDonald, for example) the Karl/Kathi relationship in *The Student Prince*. Both relationships stand out for their emotional intensity. Both couples seem perfectly matched; and in both cases the longing for consummation seems simultaneously aesthetic and sexual: hence the equation of sex with ceremony (i.e. both films have dances at their centre). Both *The Student Prince* and *The Merry Widow* therefore deal with the issue of emotional and sexual integrity. Will Karl and Kathi be able to maintain their relationship? Will Sonia and Danilo be able to establish theirs? The answers, "no" in the first case, "yes" in the second, are indicative of Lubitsch's finely tuned ambivalence. He may idealise love, but he understands that ideals can seldom be realised. So in *The Student Prince,* for example, Lubitsch makes it clear from the beginning that Karl and Kathi can never be anything but once-upon-a-time lovers; and time, made manifest in the death of Karl's uncle, comes inexorably between them.

In *The Merry Widow,* on the other hand, there is no such obvious and traumatic external threat. The relationship of Sonia and Danilo seems far more adult, more worldly, more self-contained; and yet Sonia and Danilo undergo a far more arduous and painful courtship. Therein lies the real emotional power of the film, a power which goes far beyond the pathos of *The Student Prince.* Kathi and Karl are doomed

The Merry Widow (Jeanette MacDonald) and the dashing Prince (Maurice Chevalier).

through no fault of their own beyond birth and station. But Sonia and Danilo are both very intelligent and feelingful people, and it is their intelligence, as employed in the service of emotional reticence, which nearly leads to emotional disaster. In other words, we see how easily even bright people can fall into emotional and perceptual traps, with only the slightest help from circumstance. And the implication, that human intelligence is not self-sufficient, is both harrowing and humbling.

The bitter-sweet comedy of errors gets fully underway at Maxim's, that elegant yet energetic Parisian bordello ("I've heard that's where a man can/See ladies dance the can-can") where Danilo goes to spend his last night before embarking on his secret mission. He is understandably eager to enjoy himself, to renew old sexual friendships ("Lolo, Cloclo, Joujou") before suffering the bonds of enforced matrimony. Yet his good humour verges on despair: hence his eagerness to start a quarrel with Count Popov, and hence his anger when Sonia, playing the part of a Maxim girl ("Fifi"), flirts with a moustachioed Turk at a nearby table. As Popov explains to Danilo, once they patch up their differences, Danilo's is a mission of "cold-blooded patriotism." The widow, Popov elaborates, "owns 52 per cent of Marshovia . . . if you like her or not, you love her." In other words, Danilo is being asked to subjugate his own emotions to the affairs of state, and he goes to Maxim's in order to experience for the last time a truly honest, emotionally-open, sort of sexuality (*Danilo:* "Did you miss me girls?" *Girls:* "Yes!" *Danilo:* "And I missed you — all of you").

Sonia goes to Maxim's for a similar reason. She goes specifically in search of Danilo, who represents, particularly by comparison with her other fortune-hunting suitors, a refreshingly honest, out-front, sexuality. He enjoys "girls, girls, girls," and Sonia is girl enough to appreciate his spirited enthusiasm: witness her Mae West imitation. Unfortunately, however, she also remains lady enough to take offense at Danilo's apparent devil-may-care attitude. To be sure, she misreads his motives; and she fails to account for the effect her own presence as "Fifi" has on Danilo's emotions and his rhetoric. She assumes, specifically, that his sudden seriousness is only a seductive ploy, when in fact his emotional haste is encouraged by his situation: he is genuinely attracted to "Fifi" — he does not recognize her as Sonia because he has never seen Sonia without her widow's veil — and he knows that their relationship can only last till morning, however much he may wish it otherwise. Furthermore, his praise of Maxim girls (who can "enjoy today without bothering about tomorrow") is clearly and specifically directed toward "Fifi," toward her ability to dance, to smile, to live life fully. Even when it is clear that she is a lady ("just one of those women who asks silly questions") he refuses to change his tune: "I wouldn't let you go for anything in the world." Sonia, however, refuses to acknowledge the legitimacy of his affection for her ("you don't even know what love is"). Sonia can hardly be blamed for her reticence here, particularly as her reactions are based on insufficient knowledge. But we nevertheless regret the fact that she lets fear overcome attraction; she extrapolates motives from Danilo's behaviour which run directly counter to the emotional honesty so brilliantly expressed in and embodied by their dance. Thus Sonia projects her own fear of involvement on to Danilo and refuses to accept dancing as sufficient proof of emotional sincerity.

The error is compounded at the embassy ball where both lovers come

Sonia and Danilo are formally introduced as Count Popov (Edward Everett Horton) looks on conspiratorially.

to false conclusions about themselves and their relationship. Danilo, of course, is there only reluctantly, and only because he had been too drunk to distinguish between the Marshovian Embassy and Maxim's. He is in love with "another woman," he tells the Ambassador, and he refuses, between cups of black coffee, to "make love to that widow." His reluctance is quickly overcome, however, when "Fifi" makes her entrance: there is an exchange of close-ups, revealing recognition, distrust, and longing, accompanied by Edward Everett Horton's absurdly beside-the-point social chatter ("well, what a surprise, Captain Danilo, well of all people"). In other words, the scene "happens" at several levels. Horton even assumes that Sonia and Danilo are talking in code; but their conversation, however oblique in its implications,

63

represents a genuine attempt to get to the emotional heart of the matter.

Getting to the heart of the matter, however, is no easy task. Danilo tries to bridge the gap, admits that he has fallen "madly" in love "with a girl"; and he asserts, as a consequence, that he does not "jump over garden walls anymore." Sonia, too, admits a change of heart, though it is not necessarily a change for the better: "Fifi is no more. You killed her. After she left you last night she came home and committed suicide – she jumped into a cold bath." Once again we see Sonia's reticence at work. Like Danilo, she longs for a lasting relationship, but her first such relationship ended in emotional disaster, her husband's death, and she is understandably reluctant to risk a similar episode. She is as honest as she can be in this ("You'd be surprised, Captain, what cold water can do"), and it is her obvious seriousness that encourages Danilo to continue the discussion despite Sonia's discouraging stance. Nevertheless every assertion of love on his part only meets with increasing scepticism on Sonia's, a scepticism all the stronger for each of the many fortune hunters who have followed her to the ball: "what could it be – is it my charm, or my beauty, or . . . do you suppose it's my position?" At which point Danilo begins to doubt *her* intentions, to evidence his own brand of emotional reticence. He answers her question by asserting that "it was strictly the money" he was after, and by wondering aloud whether her motive for going to Maxim's was a rich woman's desire for cheap thrills.

We know otherwise: therefore our anxiety when we see both of them playing so expertly at scepticism. Again, we have a scene taking place at several levels. On the surface, Sonia and Danilo seem disgusted with each other; but at a deeper level it is clear, at least to us, that their anger only serves to mask genuine and powerful feelings. They obviously care very much for each other – they would hardly quarrel so elaborately and with so much emotional finesse were it otherwise – and hence the emotional release which accompanies the subsequent playing of the "Merry Widow Waltz." As Nancy Schwartz put it in "Film Comment": "The music cuts right through to their true emotions and desires."[8] Put another way, the music symbolises – it *is* – their relationship at its most genuine and legitimate level. It represents that stream of pure, unfettered emotional movement which flows beneath the stormy surface of their love affair. When the music starts, they forget their anger, and are drawn together by a sensual force "against which they are helpless."[8]

Unfortunately, as dances will, the dance comes to an end, and Sonia and Danilo are forced to maintain their delicate emotional balance without the assistance of the music. Sonia's anger has melted, but

Danilo's sincerity remains an issue. Sonia asks if he still likes Maxim girls? Danilo replies: "I love you, and only you darling, please believe me." Sonia does "believe" him, after a fashion, but her belief, like her earlier disbelief, is motivated by her own emotional requirements: "I do believe you, because I want to believe you." Sonia still allows her feelings to dictate her perceptions, and hence the delicate balance of hope and fear, love and hate, is all the more delicate, all the more vulnerable to slight shifts of feeling or circumstance. Thus, while we are justified in downplaying the significance of Marshovian politics, those politics are nevertheless important, not for themselves, but for the effect they have on Sonia and Danilo.

It is not a matter, as it was in *The Student Prince,* of overpowering circumstance upsetting an otherwise stable relationship. The Sonia/Danilo relationship is far from stable, and therefore even insignificant shifts in circumstance are magnified in their effect. So, for example, when Popov is forced by press leaks to announce prematurely "the coming marriage and present engagement" of Sonia and Danilo, Sonia's immediate reaction is one of renewed scepticism: "How does he know? How does anyone know except you and me?" That scepticism is only reinforced when she overhears Popov upbraid Danilo for "giving away a government secret to a lot of Maxim girls." As Popov puts it: "if the widow ever finds out that this is a conspiracy, that the government sent you here, she'll call off the marriage." Sonia has feared all along that Danilo was merely playing with her emotions, and now her worst fear seems confirmed. Furthermore, her love for Danilo, as she points out at his treason trial, is proof positive of his duplicity. His mission was to win her heart, he won it, and therefore he carried out his cold-blooded orders to the letter: "I know it, and the Maxim girls, all Paris, the whole world knows you love me — and everybody knows . . . why." Again she misreads his motives — and his actions. Specifically, she disregards, firstly, the fact that he did not know she was the merry widow when he first became involved with her (he loves her for herself, not her money), and secondly, that he was about to tell her the truth, of his own accord, out of genuine regard for her feelings, *before* she cut him off by showing him the open transom window. In other words, his sincerity is genuine, but she chooses to ignore the facts. Her refusal is motivated by fear, and in her fear she seizes upon the flimsiest evidence that circumstance provides to justify her irrational, self-destructive, actions. Her behaviour verges on hysteria, and her hysterical laughter as she dances with the "gentlemen" confirms this reading.

What must happen, then, in order for Danilo and Sonia to cement their relationship, is an easing-up of circumstance and the re-assertion of positive emotional value: which dictates, practically speaking, a return to Marshovia. Paris, for all of its marvellous energy, is too evanescent, things happen too quickly, situations change at dangerously short notice; and amateur Parisians, like Sonia, are incapable of assuming a solid, responsible emotional stance in the midst of so much movement. Danilo's trial, therefore, provides Sonia with opportunity both to return to Marshovia and to see Danilo again. Indeed, were she genuinely antagonistic she would not return, not testify, and would let Danilo rot in jail. Her decision to testify, therefore, is evidence of her concern, and her testimony, wherein she admits her love for Danilo, is further evidence of her feelings. She couches her testimony in the rhetoric of outrage ("he lied, he deceived me, he played with emotion, romance"), but the implications are clear ("he was willing to break a woman's heart"). Similarly in Danilo's case: he almost willingly accepts arrest as a means of leaving Paris and Sonia behind. His testimony at the trial – pleading guilty to "being a fool: for once in my life I lost both my heart and my head" – only re-affirms the bond between them. Even in anger they are very much alike, ironic, self-possessed, and defensive.

Clearly both Sonia and Danilo sense their emotional unity. It must be as obvious to them as it is to us that their mutual defensiveness only hides more genuine feelings. This accounts, surely, for Sonia's decision to visit Danilo in prison; and it accounts as well for the fact that their reconciliation is so effortless, and feels so right. Indeed, the final scene in Danilo's cell recalls, in its elegant simplicity, its precision, its honesty, the scene in Danilo's private dining-room at Maxim's – but the emotional situation is far less strained. Sonia is no longer playing an uncomfortable sexual role, and Danilo is no longer part of a distasteful sexual conspiracy. If anything, Danilo is now one with Sonia in being the victim of such a conspiracy. The king has locked the door on Danilo's cell, trapping the two of them alone together, and freedom can only be regained through marriage.

But putting it that way, as if marriage were a matter of entrapment, ignores the fact that both Sonia and Danilo welcome the circumstance. For once, events have conspired in their favour, so as to reinforce their affections rather than their fears. Indeed, were it not for the locked door, Sonia might have walked out in a final fit of jealousy (Danilo had been invited to a party in the women's ward of the prison); but once the door is locked, Sonia very quickly gets into the spirit of things. The two of them trade self-aware, self-mocking quips; and the gypsy fiddlers start to play the "Merry Widow Waltz," – the aural representation of the feelings and experiences which bind them together in love. Thus it is no surprise at all when the priest pokes his head through the door to

One last attempt at escape—but King Achmed has locked the door.

conduct the ceremony. Indeed, Sonia and Danilo have already exchanged wedding vows.

> Sonia: Any man who can dance through life
> with hundreds of women . . .
> Danilo: And is willing to walk through life
> with one . . . should be . . . married.

Thus the priest hardly gets started before Danilo says "certainly" and Sonia "of course."

The Merry Widow ends, then, on a note of perfect frivolity. What we hoped for comes marvellously to pass. In this respect *The Merry Widow* seems out of step with films such as *The Student Prince* and *The Man I*

The upper class and its image: *Three Women* and *Madame DuBarry*.

Killed, films in which the demands of society and the yearnings of the heart seem very much, and very irrevocably, at odds. All three films end in marriage, either solemnised or implied, but only in *The Merry Widow* does the marriage fulfill our legitimate and hopeful expectations. Indeed, the merry widow's marriage seems to solve all problems, personal and social. That is, social and personal well-being are one and the same, and are perfectly symbolised by marriage, at once a personal and social estate. Frivolity and responsibility are therefore perfectly balanced, perfectly aligned; and Marshovian society, as embodied by the king and his courtiers who gather outside Danilo's cell, participates in celebrating the joyful occasion.

Indeed, *The Merry Widow* can best be understood as ceremony rather than analysis. The earlier films, i.e. *The Marriage Circle, Lady Windermere's Fan, The Student Prince,* are realistic and satiric, focusing on the disassociation between social and personal necessities. Furthermore they focus on an upper-class, before-the-crash boredom. *The Marriage Circle,* in particular, is about people with no real social duties, people who spend their days spinning out elaborate schemes and dreams of sexual passion. Theirs was an age of ease and irresponsibility, and Lubitsch approached their upper-class ethos with an appropriate sense of scepticism. He clearly had his doubts regarding the genuine significance of ivory-fan anxieties, doubts which the depression could not help but reinforce. Thus it is not surprising that Lubitsch's post-crash films came to attach ever-increasing significance to more basic, less class-bound, aspects of human behaviour. In this light, then, *The Merry Widow* is a myth in the best sense of the word, as an assertion of *should be,* as a personal/social ideal, something to strive for. Life is never perfect. Even Marshovia, after all, is on the verge of bankruptcy. And Lubitsch does not offer marriage as a social cure-all. In fact, he keeps the film's action in a realm of stylised fantasy far enough removed from reality to maintain the distinction. Lubitsch makes it clear that personal and social harmony *is* a fantasy, but it nevertheless remains meaningful as an image of the possible. We must keep in mind, as well, how tenuous even fantasy solutions can be. The Sonia/Danilo relationship is agonised in the extreme: suffering is universal, regardless of class, and alleviating that suffering is never simple or easy. Even a splendid film like *The Merry Widow* could offer only a moment of gaiety in the midst of world-wide sadness.

3 Self-Aware Illusions: One Hour with You (1932), Trouble in Paradise (1932), and To Be or Not To Be (1942)

The one significant generalisation that seems to hold good across the entire Lubitsch canon is that, in his films, Lubitsch plays with and reflects upon distinctions between fact and fantasy, between reality and illusion, between "l'être et le paraître."[9] I cannot think of a single Lubitsch film within the realm of my experience where this illusion/ reality antinomy is not at work to one degree or another. If I have chosen to focus for the most part on other aspects of the Lubitsch vision it is for the simple reason that this duality of fact and fiction seems readily apparent, to viewers in general, and certainly to other critics (see Gerald Mast, for example). Nevertheless, if this discussion is to be genuinely representative of Lubitsch in America, we must pay some attention to this very important, very typical, though not necessarily simple aspect of the Lubitsch cinema. For brevity's sake, however, I will focus on three films which play particularly upon the disjunction between "is" and "seems": *One Hour with You*, *Trouble in Paradise*, and *To Be or Not To Be*.

* * *

One Hour with You appears, on the surface at least, one of Lubitsch's most trivial films, particularly when compared to its predecessor, *The Marriage Circle*. Both films share the same basic

"What a little thing like a wedding ring can do": Jeanette MacDonald and Maurice Chevalier in *One Hour with You.*

mistaken-identity plot, but the emphasis clearly shifts from the cynical couple (The Professor and Mizzi) to the less cynical lovers (André and Colette in *One Hour*). Indeed, *One Hour with You* opens and closes with André and Colette. It is clearly their world, lacking any real sense of tragedy. If anything, seriousness seems subsumed by an easy-going sense of intimacy. Indeed, characters can talk directly to us. We become, in fact, their confidants. André (Chevalier) in particular seems an ally, and in his moments of fun and frustration he just naturally turns to us, speaking directly into the camera, either to share his elation or to confide his sorrows. Furthermore, the better we get to know these characters, the less worried we are about what happens to them. They

71

are far more self-aware, far more sexually aware, than their predecessors in *The Marriage Circle*. They may make mistakes, they may even complicate their mistakes; but we know that when the party is over they will have learned their lesson, and will have the common sense and good manners necessary to patch up their differences and resume their proper places in the upper-class scheme of things. These characters are, then, with perhaps one major exception, in control of themselves.

The only character who gets significantly out of control is Adolph, Colette's would-be paramour, who routinely lets his burning passion override his sense of decorum. But, again significantly, Adolph (as played by Charlie Ruggles) is the only character who engages our deeper sympathies, and then only briefly. For once in his life he musters the courage necessary for seduction, taking advantage of André's absence (André is off with Mitzi) to reveal his own deep and abiding passion for Colette (Jeanette MacDonald). And when his attempt fails, when Colette orders him out, he hangs his head, twiddles his fingers, picks up his hat and his coat, and walks dejectedly to the door. Sympathy is obviously the proper response here, both on our part and on Colette's, and she, in her gentle good sense, does not disappoint us. She ties Adolph's tie as he walks out, a gesture both kind and decorous, and his sense of self-worth is rejuvenated.

Unlike Adolph, however, Lubitsch has things well under control.[10] Indeed, when we start to investigate the artifice of *One Hour with You,* looking beyond surface laughter to the aesthetic structure, we begin to realise that the film is well aware of its own frivolity, for it constantly provides an internal critique of its own folly. Consider, for example, the last tango scene at the dinner party (which recalls, in no small detail, the dinner scene in *The Marriage Circle*). During the meal itself Colette throws silent, dagger-like glances at André, thinking (with Mitzi's encouragement) that André has been romancing Mlle. Martelle. Then, after the meal, all move to the dance floor, and we get a sequence of duets, each mismatched couple singing some version of "One Hour with You." First we see Mitzi (who has cut in on Mlle. Martelle) trying to seduce André, moving her eyebrows suggestively in time with her musical *double entendres.* Lubitsch then cuts immediately to Colette and Adolph, and, to our pleasant surprise, Adolph starts singing his own hilarious though pathetic swansong. Once again our response is one with Colette's, a bemused, sympathetic bewilderment that so unromantic a fellow could want so much to be a Romeo. More importantly, however, the juxtaposition of one duet with the next serves to puncture, at least for us, the overblown seriousness of the situation. André is no more likely to cheat on Colette, whether it be with Mitzi or Mlle. Martelle, than Colette is likely to cheat on André by falling seriously for Adolph. It's simply beyond belief (André never believes it). Thus Lubitsch is able to encompass our disbelief within the range of legitimate response: it's perfectly appropriate that we question the believability of what we see, and it is appropriate because seeing and believing are the film's primary concerns, both in terms of plot and theme.

Of course, sex is clearly the underlying motivation for everything in *One Hour with You.* It makes people do the things they do (as is almost always the case in comedy), but they do those things in a particular way because they live in a set of upper-class circumstances (circumstances seen elsewhere in Lubitsch) where appearances carry the weight of social relationships, for good or ill. Thus the film's intrigue gets started when Colette mistakes appearance for reality. She and André are in bed (he can make love anywhere, as *she* tells us in the preceeding scene); and while he wants to get down to the reality of sex, she wants to talk about the next day's luncheon guest. André, naturally enough, does not care to discuss the next day's luncheon, particularly when there are more pressing physical and emotional issues to deal with. We must note, then, how Colette interprets what goes on. Rather than understand the sexual imperatives of the situation, she chooses to believe that André bears ill-will against their next day's guest, Colette's old school-chum Mitzi. Colette takes it personally, so that André's turning off the bedside light becomes, for her, evidence of rejection rather than affection. It is perfectly clear, however, that André has nothing at all against Mitzi: he was turning the light off long before Mitzi's name was ever mentioned. But once the bulb starts to flick on and off, once he and Colette start to quarrel about what to do and when to do it and with whom, he does have something against Mitzi. He has never met the lady, but already she interferes with his sex life. He has something against Colette as well: she doesn't know when to shut up and make love (and don't forget that it was Colette's idea to go to bed in the first place). What happens, then, is that appearance *becomes* reality. Colette's false assumption, that André has something against Mitzi, becomes true as she persists in her belief. Hence the danger of getting appearance and reality so readily confused.

The reason that Colette can confuse the two is that she lacks a proper sense of scepticism, the sort of scepticism that the film encourages in its audience. In fact, *One Hour with You* is a movie which playfully questions the veracity of movies, for it invites us to question what we see. Often, for example, we will witness an action, then André will turn around and explain it to us directly, as if we are not to trust the images alone. Consider the moment when fumble-fingers André is caught with his bow-tie untied on the veranda. Either he goes inside and asks Colette to tie it, at which point she will wonder how it became untied; or he follows Mitzi, who untied it in the first place, into the garden, which would not look any better for André than walking around in public with his tie hanging loose. The situation could not be much clearer – Catch 22 – but André feels compelled to explain it to us nevertheless. Colette gets into trouble, then, because she places

André (Chevalier) and Mitzi (Genevieve Tobin) get a breath of fresh air in *One Hour with You*.

too much trust in what she sees, too little in what she hears (appropriately enough in a musical). As she tells André just before the dinner party, when she catches him rearranging the name cards (he wants to avoid sitting next to Mitzi), she would not believe the truth if he told it to her. And later, after the party, when he tries to tell her the truth once again, she adamantly refuses to believe or accept it: she saw what she saw (André getting his tie tied).

But we know what she really saw, and what she saw was the work of a master illusionist. Mitzi was the one, of course, who directed that party scene, who manipulated appearances with the skill necessary to make her seduction of André appear to Colette as the rescue of André. Thus Colette worries about André and Mlle. Martelle while ignoring completely the possibility that anything might be afoot between André and Mitzi herself. For the moment, then, Mitzi has the upper hand, and André is caught by Catch 22 again: he cannot help but look unfaithful. He either agrees to Mitzi's proposal or rejects her altogether, at which point Mitzi convinces Colette that André has an affair going with Mlle. Martelle.

Of course, beyond some routine if enjoyable hugging and kissing, André does not betray his wife. He never once stops loving her, despite her foolishness, and his willingness to spend that one evening with Mitzi is not motivated by any grand passion for Mitzi but by frustration with Colette's stupidity. Furthermore, we feel that he is perfectly justified in his actions. As he tells us in one of his songs, he is only human after all, and what he does is the human thing to do, particularly when what he does is hardly reprehensible.

And it is the humanness of it all that is both Lubitsch's point and the means whereby plot issues are resolved. At the film's conclusion Colette goes into her wronged-wife routine, weeping and crying divorce. Then Adolph makes his timely if coincidental entrance, at which point André finally gets *his* chance to direct the scene, his chance to manipulate appearances; which he does rather successfully. He encourages Adolph, by gesturing to him while Colette's back is turned, to admit his passion for, and his impropriety with, Colette. Thus she gets the chance to play the woman-of-the-world role (as a comical means of revenging herself on André), and André reciprocates by playing the wronged-husband role: appearances thus are equalised. At the film's conclusion, then, both agree that "to err is human" and that to forgive human beings their humanity is certainly the humane thing to do. Thus we get a sort of comic levelling, which includes, ultimately, the audience as well as the characters. The last moment of the film finds Colette and André speaking directly to us, asking what we would have done in their situation, and telling us that they did it too. All human beings are equal, therefore, in their capacity for folly, not only André and Colette, but ourselves as well.

This does not necessarily mean that we are not responsible for our actions, that the Professor (Mitzi's husband) is correct in asserting that no one is guilty because "our doings are controlled by circumstances over which we have no control." For, as the Professor also says, that theory has "nothing to do with our case." Again it is a matter of our humanity.

Just what the patient ordered—the doctor.

We should not feel guilty about being human, at least to the extent that being human involves certain natural imperatives such as sex. People should not feel guilty about their sexuality (*Ninotchka* makes much the same point). They should, however, take care how they exercise that sexuality, how they deal with social situations and with each other. Sex is no sin, but neither is it an excuse for irresponsible behaviour.

This takes us back to the appearance/reality issue. The most reprehensible character in the film, the one must responsible for what little pain people suffer, is Colette, the character who pays the least attention to the implications (particularly the sexual implications) of her actions and assumptions. Colette is a generally pleasant person, but a person insufficiently sceptical. She thinks she has things under control, and does not. The most admirable character, in turn, is André, and André because he is the most sceptical about appearances and the most capable of attending to their implications. André does not assume that appearance is reality (he is never fooled by Mitzi), and therefore he can manipulate appearances in order to bring people to their senses. André can make people aware of their own short-comings without humiliating or offending them.

Which is exactly what Lubitsch does in *One Hour with You*. He manipulates appearances in order to bring us to our comic senses. We see the kinds of mistakes that people can make, the sort of perceptual and emotional traps that even good-intentioned folk can fall into, and hence we are better prepared to avoid such traps ourselves. We should never take ourselves too seriously; and we cannot take life, in all of its marvellous frivolity and complexity, seriously enough.

* * *

Trouble in Paradise locates itself midway between the somewhat bitter social satire of *Lady Windermere's Fan* and the essentially good-hearted grace of *One Hour with You*. Both of the earlier films posit a world of highly-polished social surfaces which serve to mask more eventful personal realities. In *Lady Windermere's Fan*, however, the contrast is clearly satiric, bitingly so, and society's tendency to prefer propriety over genuine feeling is clearly taken to task. In *One Hour with You*, on the other hand, genuine feeling is given full expression. If anything, Colette almost welcomes the opportunity to imagine her husband unfaithful, and by so doing she expresses a genuine longing for extraordinary sexual excitement. It is all in good, prurient fun; and no one is really hurt. Thus the society in *One Hour with You* legitimately escapes condemnation; whereas society in *Lady Windermere's Fan* comes under close satiric scrutiny.

Some critics, most notably Gerald Mast and Richard Koszarski, bear down heavily on the satiric aspects of *Trouble in Paradise*, seeing in it the same sort of social indignation which motivates the satire in *Lady Windermere's Fan*. The film, says Koszarski, "relates a series of sex/money metaphors against a background of times so troubled that the true nature of anything is suspect."[11] For example, our gondolier is a garbage man, our Baron a jewel thief, and our Countess a cutpurse. Indeed, as Mast puts it, even the rich are thieves "in that they are frivolous with money that could fill a family table."[12]

Seen from this perspective, then, the film's satire is a function of inverted probabilities, of inverted values. *Trouble in Paradise* thus approaches the appearance/reality issue in terms not of the deluded, those like Colette in *One Hour with You* who jump to false, self-serving conclusions, who cannot keep appearance and reality straight; but in terms of the illusionists, those masters of deception, like the legendary jewel-thief, Gaston Monescu (Herbert Marshall), who self-consciously manipulate appearances in the service of their own marvellously

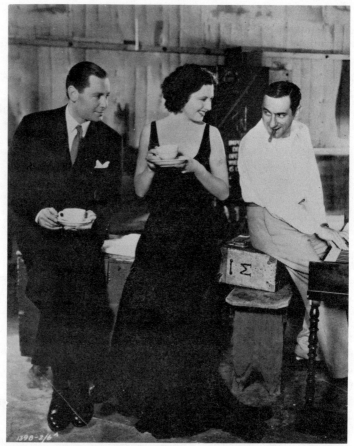

Tea time in paradise: Herbert Marshall, Kay Francis, and Ernst Lubitsch.

improbable designs for living. Monescu, indeed, is comic improbability personified. He can do the impossible with grace and *sang-froid*. There is seemingly nothing he cannot steal, except perhaps peace itself, and there is no situation that he cannot talk his way out of. Furthermore, his particular trade, thievery, strikes at the very heart of the superficial capitalist social system, for he disregards all notion of private property. With Monescu about, no one can be secure in the probability of possession. That probability becomes all the more tenuous when Gaston allies his talents with those of Lily (Miriam Hopkins), the slinky false Countess of Venice. Like Gaston, she has a sharp wit, a quick tongue, and a deft touch. Anyone who can pick Monescu's pocket successfully has, by definition, transcended the probable.

This Gaston/Lily pair is set against the generally self-important slow-tongued aristocracy of the old world. Gaston and Lily prey upon those like Monsieur Fileba (Edward Everett Horton), and even Madame Colet (another merry widow), who trust overmuch to probability. That is, Gaston and Lily prey upon those who trust what they see and hear. Thus Gaston and his polished manners always pass inspection, and always gain entrance to the haunts of the rich. Gaston is the master of the improbable because he is master of the probable: he knows what people expect in given social situations, and what they will put up with. He knows that Fileba, for example, will take ten minutes to talk about tonsils; and while such victims listen to his charming small talk, Gaston takes them for all their insurance companies are worth.

Thus another assault on probability is the fact that, in this film, the rich are the victims, both of Gaston's thievery, and Lubitsch's satire. We know, of course, that wealth does buy happiness, contrary to popular assumption, and that real poverty can purchase little but misery. In *Trouble in Paradise,* however, things are a bit different. The most miserable people we see are Fileba and Madame Colet (Kay Francis). And the very fact of their misery, however improbable it might be, is emphasised by being set against the very real pain of the poor during the depression. As Gaston tells us, times are hard, so hard that everyone, Gaston included, should carry only cash.

The fact of hard times is also underlined the first time we see Madame Colet. She is at a board meeting of Colet and Co., perfume manufacturers ("It doesn't matter how you look, it's how you smell"), and she listens to Giron, long-time head of her board of directors, as he suggests a pay cut as a means of riding out the financial storm in good shape (to her credit she pleads boredom and instructs Giron to "leave the salaries just where they are"). But the most poignant contrast between rich and poor comes after Madame Colet has lost (with Gaston's help) her impulsively-purchased, diamond-encrusted, 125,000-franc purse. She advertises in the press, offering a 20,000 franc reward. Cut then to the Colet mansion, where we see a briefly held long shot of Madame Colet's expansive parlour, an elegant room full of inelegant people, all hoping they have the enchanted purse. Then we get a brief two-shot of Madame Colet and a poor little old lady as Madame hands back a beaded and bedraggled old hand-bag. The moment is fleeting, and our sympathy for the poor woman is interrupted by the comically-played Trotsky-spouting Bolshevik, but the point is made. For every rich lady upstairs there is many a poor one down below.

Furthermore, as Gaston himself tells us, the *vieux* poor, those who have been poor for their entire lifetimes, are now being joined by the *nouveau* poor, those made paupers by the sudden stock-market crash: poverty flourishes.

To some extent, then, the trouble in paradise is that glaring poverty and luxurious wealth exist side by side; and the wealthy, the only people capable of bridging the misery gap, seem completely blind to the reality of misfortune and social injustice. All the rich seem to see is their own enclosed universe of opera houses, dinner parties, and golf

M. Fileba (Edward Everett Horton) and the Major (Charlie Ruggles) shopping for baubles in *Trouble in Paradise*.

courses. The rich, in fact, seem to live in a Hollywood daydream, an elegant place constructed by the Paramount art department, a place where kings and queens can gossip while garbage floats by unnoticed.

Thus another strong element of the film is the satire, not only of the rich, but of the romantic conventions which rich people indulge. You must be rich, like Monsieur Fileba, to occupy rooms 253, 5, 7, and 9, and to enjoy the companionship of high-class female "business associates" as well. You must be rich to sit in an opera box, to buy expensive handbags; and you must at least appear to be rich, as Gaston and Lily appear to be, to indulge the luxury of histrionic gestures, extravagant poses, and an elegant meal over which to reveal one's true vocation. Thus the initial rendezvous between Gaston and Lily provides a magnificent triple perspective on the games rich people play. That is, Gaston and Lily are poor people (their assets are their abilities, not their bank accounts), who pretend to be rich people, who in turn are pretending to be Hollywood movie stars (Miriam Hopkins and Herbert Marshall, perhaps). The scene is thus an hilarious parody to the third power; and our laughter is all the more intense, and all the more pointed, as we realise that the Baron is a thief and the Countess a pickpocket. We remember the way Lily threw herself in mock despair on to the sofa at the thought that her honourably naughty assignation would become only one more piece of Grand Canal gossip. We remember Gaston's request for "moon" in the champagne. We recall Lily riding like Cleopatra in her gondola. And we sense that convention is merely a mask for self-indulgence, however glorious that self-indulgence might be.

But we have left something out. Something else takes place in that rendezvous scene, and in the film in general, which greatly modifies our critique. For all of its satiric touches, as marvellous and numerous as they may be, *Trouble in Paradise* goes beyond satire and achieves an unexpected depth of emotional involvement.

If we look again at the Gaston/Lily rendezvous, we find that the truth of their characters finally does emerge.

> *Lily:* Please, when I came here it was for a little adventure, a little game in which you play tonight and forget tomorrow. Something's changed me; and it isn't the champagne. The whole thing is so new to me. I have a confession to make to you. Baron, you are a crook. You robbed the gentleman in 253, 5, 7 and 9.
>
> *(Gaston passes the salt)*
>
> . . .

81

Gaston: Countess, believe me, before you left this room I would have told you everything. And let me say this with love in my heart. Countess, you are a thief. The wallet of the gentleman in 253, 5, 7, and 9 is in your possession. I knew it very well when you took it out of my pocket. In fact, you tickled me. But your embrace was so sweet.

(Gaston leaves the table to lock the door and pull the curtains. He then pulls Lily violently to her feet and shakes her—until the wallet falls to the floor)

. . .

Lily: What time is it? *(She allows him to search for his watch before handing it to him.)* It was five minutes slow but I regulated it for you.

Gaston: I hope you don't mind if I keep your garter. *(She checks her leg, under the table, and then Gaston holds the garter up to prove his expertise).*

Lily: Darling! *(excitedly)* Tell me, tell me all about yourself. Who are you?

What was to be an evening's light adventure suddenly becomes a very serious meeting of two like-minded souls. Like Sonia and Danilo, Lily and Gaston are clearly meant for each other. They are absolute equals in wit and ability (witness the above); and hence honesty, a truly open emotional and intellectual honesty, is suddenly not only possible but necessary: they cannot fool each other.

But it is not simply a matter of *cannot,* of not being able to play games. They rather delight in each other's presence and have no desire to play at dishonesty. At which point, then, those Hollywood conventions no longer seem so silly. Gaston can hover over Lily, whispering sweet nothings in her ear, and she can lean melodramatically back on the couch, without either of them being insincere. Of course, Gaston does not compliment a non-existent beauty (although she is beautiful). Instead he compliments her on her abilities as a thief, calling her his "little shoplifter," his "sweet little pickpocket," and so forth. So what this scene in particular and the film in general hold out for is not the destruction of convention, or tradition, or society. It is not a matter of flat-out condemnation. On the contrary, as in *One Hour with You,* Lubitsch holds out for the re-invigoration of conventions, injecting a sufficient dose of honesty and self-awareness into otherwise dying but nevertheless valuable social institutions. Lubitsch would be the last man on earth to advocate the destruction of perfume factories.

This intention explains, then, the otherwise inexplicable affair between Madame Colet and Gaston. If rich people were by definition

The thief (Herbert Marshall) woos the widow (Kay Francis).

bad people, then Madame Colet would not count, and her relationship with Gaston would be similarly insignificant. But, with the exception of Giron, whose sanctimonious facade serves only to mask the embezzler beneath, we like the rich people in the film. They are human, just as the characters in *One Hour with You* are human. They even shave sitting on the edge of the bathtub in their drawers on occasion. And what Lubitsch is concerned to do is to show us how their salvation can come about.

What happens, then, is simple; Madame Colet, much to her surprise, suddenly comes to understand the reality of poverty. Of course, she will never know financial hardship even in hard times, but she can

Lily (Miriam Hopkins) confronts Gaston with his infidelity in *Trouble in Paradise.*

experience emotional deprivation. She genuinely loves the Gaston she knows, is willing to ruin her reputation and his to consumate that love; but she discovers her lover to be a crook, discovers that he loves someone else as well as herself, and that circumstances (the imminent prospect of Gaston's arrest) prevent her from ever sharing life with Gaston no matter how much she (or Gaston, for that matter) yearns to do so. In other words, she is forced, suddenly, to look quite honestly at herself and her somewhat illusory life. To her great credit she does so, willingly letting Gaston leave, willingly parting with that necklace as a gift of sorts to Lily; and thus she willingly admits that her previously comfortable view of life is no longer sufficient.

Thus Madame Colet learns a lesson. And so too do Gaston and Lily come to a deeper awareness — both of themselves and of human relationships generally. Thus Gaston discovers the seemingly improbable truth that rich folks are human beings too — people who can give love and who are worth loving in return. Thus Lily discovers that she cannot rest assured on the probability that Gaston is hers and hers alone. Life is always touched by improbability; nothing is as sure as it seems; and having that "Lubitsch touch" means having a real appreciation of life's marvellous absurdity, a genuine and self-aware appreciation of the countless ways in which reality can (and must) step in to upset shopworn conventions of behaviour and belief.

* * *

To Be or Not to Be continues Lubitsch's comic investigation of the relationship between illusion and reality. As we have seen in our discussion of *One Hour with You* and *Trouble in Paradise,* Lubitsch is

The blue-blood barber (Jack Buchanan) woos his dream princess (Jeanette MacDonald) in *Monte Carlo.*

85

partial to actors. Indeed, his method of directing actors was to act out their parts himself; and characters of the Mitzi/Gaston sort aroused admiration and respect precisely for their ability to manipulate the probability of appearances. Lubitsch had taken the illusion/reality antinomy to the logical extreme before. In *Monte Carlo* there is a scene in which Jeanette MacDonald, in love with a blueblood who pretends to be a barber, watches an operetta which is *about* a woman in love with a blueblood who pretends to be a barber: art and life once again come into close alignment. *Design for Living* also reflects upon the interplay between fact (Edward Everett Horton's impassioned declaration that "immorality may be fun but it isn't enough to take the place of one hundred per cent virtue and three square meals a day") and dramatic fiction (the Fredric March character, Tom, uses the line in his play "Goodnight Bassington"). In *To Be or Not To Be,* however, Lubitsch raises the life/art issue more explicitly than ever before. Indeed, as Graham Petrie points out, *"To Be or Not To Be* emerges as the most 'modern' of all Lubitsch's films" precisely because it anticipates films such as *Last Year in Marienbad* in which all distinctions between "fact, dream, hallucination, memory, desire, fear, and foreboding" cease to operate.[13] Given insufficient clues, audiences are forced to take all images at their immediate face value: all images are equally 'real' on the screen.

We see something of this in *To Be or Not To Be.* Almost all of the sympathetic characters are actors of one sort or another, members of the Theatre Polski, and the film begins with an elaborate cinematic deception. We see a bustling Warsaw street, people, cars, sidewalk cafés, when suddenly the activity comes to a jarring and unexpected halt. As the voice-over narrator puts it: "Everybody seems to be staring in one direction; people seem frightened, even terrified, some are flabbergasted. Can it be true? It must be true, no doubt. The man with the little moustache, Adolf Hitler." The narrator then proceeds to explain Hitler's presence in peace-time Warsaw by taking us where "it all started," the "general headquarters of the Gestapo in Berlin." Jack Benny is seated behind a desk, in full Gestapo regalia, a young Hitler youth is called in, and is bribed with a toy tank to inform against his father. The interrogation is suddenly interrupted, however, by the entrance of the Fuhrer, in person. Everyone "heil Hitlers," and then Herr Hitler, out of the blue, "heils" himself. We cut then to the theatre director (Dobosh: played by Charles Halton) who rises from his chair in exasperation and complains: "that's not in the script."

Now, as Petrie has it, this abrupt and unexpected plunge "into the illusion-reality, theatre-life dichotomy that is central to the film . . . makes it impossible for us to take anything that follows on face

To Be or Not To Be: members of the Theatre Polski, including Jack Benny and Carole Lombard (center), take to the bomb shelter.

value."[13] Petrie is right, of course, to point out the centrality of the theatre-life issue, but he clearly overstates the case for confusion. Granted, *To Be or Not To Be* is a confusing film to think about (and Petrie's article is clearly a "think piece"): when plot and counterplot are abstracted from the immediate stream of images it is possible to run them together. But the images themselves, it seems to me, are not confusing at all. Even this opening sequence provides sufficient clues to its artifice. The presence of the narrator signifies "story," his mock-heroic tone of voice undercuts the "seriousness" of the scene, and the tin-type sets clearly signify "movie." We wonder how the scene will be integrated into the film, but we are not fooled. Indeed, when

"Hitler" stomps out of the theatre to prove to his sceptical director that he really does look like Hitler, his illusion promptly wilts. A little girl walks up to him, saying "May I have your autograph, Mr. Bronski?," and Bronski has no choice but to take the autograph book and sign it.

Neither film nor theatre, it should be clear, are life. At best they are analogues, significantly related, but not identical. Thus the spear-carrier's desire to play Shylock does not derive from any confusion as to Shylock's mode of reality. It derives, rather, from a recognition of Shylock's significance. Shylock's attitude in the Realto speech embodies a vision of the world, and to value the lines is to share the vision, to feel its relevancy (thus it is significant that the Nazis do not recognise the lines). But such a feeling does not require ignorance of Shylock's theatrical origins. It must be kept in mind, therefore, that the "reality" of a film is a function of the film audience. We grant credibility by "suspending our disbelief." We recognize the analogous nature of the art/life relationship, and our sense of "film reality" is more a matter of internal consistency than simple verisimilitude. If *To Be or Not To Be* confuses (I do not believe it does), it confuses by shifting too quickly from one level of fictitiousness to another. We never shift from art to life — unless the projector breaks down.

Indeed, were Petrie correct in asserting that "the dazzling shifts from scene to scene in which characters and settings are rarely seen performing the same function twice forces us to question . . . just what is 'real' in the world the film presents to us," then it is unlikely the film would evoke laughter. As people like Freud and Arthur Koestler point out, laughter derives from recognition: we "get" a joke when we understand its converging contexts.[14] Thus Josef Tura's indignant outburst — "it's a conspiracy, that's what it is, a foul conspiracy" — is only funny because we recognise a shift in context. At first we believe that Tura's "it" refers to the German invasion, but we laugh at the discovery that Tura is talking about something else altogether, about having Lieutenant Sobinski (Robert Stack) walk out on Tura's "To be or not to be" soliloquy two nights running (the soliloquy is Sobinski's cue to meet Maria Tura backstage).

I discuss the point at length because understanding it is central to understanding Lubitsch. Lubitsch continually plays with the illusion/ reality dichotomy, but not ultimately to confuse the two. Lubitsch is far more concerned to demonstrate the necessity for keeping things in perspective. As already noted, Lubitsch almost never fools *us*. He rather shows us the foolishness of characters who fail to keep appearance and reality in appropriate balance. So, for example, the Jack Benny character, Josef Tura, "that great, great Polish actor," repeatedly allows

Jack Benny as Josef Tura as Col. Ehrhardt interrogates Stanley Ridges as Professor Siletski in *To Be or Not To Be.*

his domestic concerns, his irritation at his wife's flirtations, to intrude upon his performances, as Hamlet, and, far more importantly, as Colonel Ehrhardt, the Gestapo Chief. Tura plays the Ehrhardt role in order to prevent Professor Siletsky (a Nazi agent) from destroying the Polish underground. Siletsky knows that Lieutenant Sobinsky and Mrs. Tura were seeing each other, and he uses the information to trip Tura into revealing his true identity: as the jealous husband. Given the extraordinary circumstances, this is clearly an inappropriate balance of action and reaction on Tura's part. For once a convincing performance is a life-or-death matter; and yet it is Tura's saving grace that he never ceases to be human. We are never fooled by his actions. Lubitsch could have had it otherwise. He could have confused illusion and reality

89

almost to the point of senselessness, as Chabrol does in *La decade prodigieuse.* Lubitsch chose, however, not to go that far in the direction of subjectivity; yet neither are we completely objective and detached. We seldom look through a character's eyes — Lubitsch does not play with our subjectivity as Hitchcock does in, say, *The Lodger* — but seldom do we look on in judgement. Lubitsch does not go to either extreme. Lubitsch is rather concerned with recognition, a state mid-way between identification and judgment. He wants us above all else to recognize human frailties and legitimately humane values: it is the essence of his humour, and the essence of empathy as well.

To understand *To Be or Not To Be,* therefore, is to recognise the humanity of the characters, of Carole Lombard's Maria Tura, her elegance, her flirtatiousness, her genuine courage and resourcefulness; of Jack Benny's Joseph Tura, his fragile masculinity, his love for the limelight, his devotion to the cause of Poland and his bed-room slippers; of Felix Bressart's Greenberg, his love of laughter ("a laugh is not to be sneezed at"), his love of Shakespeare. These characters never deceive us. We see them for what they are. We acquiesce to their petty self-deceptions because they are easily recognised and readily lived with. The Nazis, on the other hand, are dangerous precisely because we do not, perhaps cannot, know them. Like the bogus Professor Siletsky, they can, for a while at least, fool us (the only time we are really deceived at all), just as Hitler deceived the world with false promises of peace.

Furthermore, in a world where everyone is an actor of one sort or another, it really does matter what sort of role you play and your reasons for playing it. It is no coincidence that the jokes which people found offensive issue from the mouths of Nazis. In a Nazi-controlled society humour can be fatal (the satiric equation of Hitler with a piece of cheese kills several). Nazi jokes are humourless precisely because of their inhumanity. Colonel Ehrhardt's equation of play-script and people (Ehrhardt says of Tura's acting: "What he did to Shakespeare, we are doing to Poland") betrays a callousness verging on insanity.[15] The film makes perfectly clear the distinction between art and life, between fantasy (Siletsky's Nazi fantasy of a "happy" world) and actuality (the concentration camps). When war breaks out, Carole Lombard says: "War, it's really war; people are going to kill each other and be killed." Later, when Siletsky offers her the role of a spy, she refuses: "I once played a spy. It was a great success. I had wonderful notices. It was really an exciting part." *Siletsky:* "Well, wouldn't it be exciting to play it in real life." *Maria:* "But I got shot in the last act. I suppose that happens to most spies." Maria recognises here the essential difference

90

between theatre and reality. In one, risks are a matter of bad notices. In the other, a matter of life or death.

What happens in the film is very simple and not at all confusing from the audience point of view. The familiar Lubitsch universe, a world of ordinary people (Lominski, Rosanski, Posnanski, etc.) and ordinary fools (Josef and Maria Tura, *et al*), moved by ordinary passions (jealousy, vanity, insecurity), is invaded by a group of extraordinary fools bent on creating an extraordinary universe, a universe devoid of laughter, devoid of feeling, so foolish as to banish foolishness by obliterating gradations between sanity and insanity (you are either insane or dead).

Maria Tura (Carole Lombard) keeps a close and patriotic eye on the collaborating Professor Siletski (Stanley Ridges).

It is a matter of degree and perspective, of course. The ordinary fools are acceptable because they enact their folly in an ordinary fashion. They may hurt and be hurt (Tura is genuinely enraged when Sobinsky walks out on his soliloquy) but they seldom indulge in cruelty for cruelty's sake, nor do they ever carry their passion to the point of mass murder. Society thus continues (its continuity is an issue in the film: *To Be or Not To Be*) and it survives by allowing sufficient room for individual eccentricity. Thus the hams have their theatre, a place where fantasy's enactment is appropriate. This sort of social accomodation may not always be the Lubitsch case. Mrs. Erlynne is almost prevented from regaining her social position in *Lady Windermere's Fan*, for example. But in general Lubitsch does not attack society *per se* so much as social rigidity. In *To Be or Not To Be*, however, society is clearly loose enough to accomodate harmless *prima donnas* like the Turas.

Nazi society, on the other hand, is rigidity carried to its most dangerous extremes. The Nazis are like the actors, devoted to themselves and their fantasies, but they are not content to limit their fantasies to the world of the theatre. They insistently impose their vision of happiness upon those who may already be happy without National Socialism. Furthermore, as Maria points out, the Nazi method for insuring social happiness is to eliminate those who are unhappy under Nazi rule. Under the Nazis, then, extreme theatricality, outside of its proper context, becomes a genuine threat to human existence; and therefore it is both necessary and appropriate that actors should save the day. They are expert enough in the manipulation of appearances to beat the Nazis at their own theatrical game. And in this they are like other Lubitsch illusionists, like Mrs. Erlynne in *Lady Windermere's Fan*, like Rudolph in *Monte Carlo*, like Gaston in *Trouble in Paradise*, like Kralik in *The Shop Around the Corner*, in that they manipulate appearances for genuinely positive ends. The danger, then, is that illusion and reality will become so monstrously confused as to permit Nazism to come into existence at all. But within the structure of the film there is very little confusion. The actors know their proper place. .Their goal is to return to a legitimate stage (where Greenberg will finally get his chance to play Shylock). And they employ the best, indeed the only, means at their disposal to bring society back to its senses. Thus it is completely appropriate and satisfying that the film should conclude with a performance of *Hamlet*, a play of murder and revenge which litters the stage with corpses. We know full well, however, that play is play, and that a general resurrection will accompany the curtain call. The only real casualty is Tura's pride. Once again someone walks out on his soliloquy, and we know that all's right with the world.

4 Love's Parade (Uncertain Feelings): *So This Is Paris* (1926), *The Love Parade* (1929), and *Ninotchka* (1939)

Love is central to the Lubitsch universe. In *To Be or Not To Be,* for example, Josef Tura loves his wife, his slippers, and his country, though not necessarily in that order. His problem, however, is that he loves not wisely but too well; he lets his jealousy get the better of him at the wrong moment, and the slip is almost fatal. Indeed, as *The Shop Around the Corner* demonstrates, Lubitsch's later films came to place increasing emphasis on the fact of love, and love, as a fact, became increasingly an issue. Will Nicole and Michael overcome their differences in *Bluebeard's Eighth Wife?* Will Jill and Larry be reconciled in *That Uncertain Feeling?* Will Angelina dump Mario and marry the Colonel in *That Lady in Ermine?*

In the earlier films, to the contrary, love is often taken for granted. *So This Is Paris,* for example, deals, like *The Marriage Circle,* with married couples whose relationships verge on emotional/sexual stasis. Again we have a young doctor, again played by Monte Blue, married to an overly romantic and very attractive young woman. Madame Giraud (Patsy Ruth Miller) is understandably bored with her uneventful upper-class existence, and she seeks emotional refuge in the torrid sexuality of Arabian Nights fiction. Indeed, we first see her sitting demurely by the window, reading about "deep kisses," "crimson twilights," "fierce lovers," and so on. She closes the book, in "extase," and stretches her body as if she were in the final moments of orgasm.[16]

Checking the divorce statutes in *That Uncertain Feeling,* with Burgess Meredith (center left), Merle Oberon (center right), and Melvyn Douglas (far right).

This pre-occupation with the physical facts of sexuality makes it all the easier for Madame Giraud to jump to conclusions when she sees a man, apparently naked, in a window across the street. Her immediate reaction is one of horror — a repulsion based clearly on attraction — and she insists that her husband go immediately across the street to punish the man: he represents a clear and present danger to her sense of propriety and reality. Giraud somewhat reluctantly agrees, boasts as much to himself as to his wife that he'll show that naked fellow what strong stuff Paul Giraud is made of, and he tries to leave — weaponless. His wife (an expert on such combats, no doubt) stops him and hands him his cane: her "sheik" can now do battle.

Giraud's expedition here is significant for two reasons, the first having to do with his motives, the second with the subsequent course of

Madam Giraud (Patsy Ruth Miller) waxes ecstatic in *So This Is Paris.*

events. His mission, clearly, is to eliminate a sexual threat. The most significant threat to sexuality, however, is not the nude next door: it is Giraud himself. Indeed, Giraud treats his wife's sexual passion as if it were a disease. We first see him as he returns from a call. His wife has just closed her book, and her husband's entrance seems a fine opportunity to express her sexuality. She presses herself against him, leans her head back, closes her eyes, and calls him her "sheik well loved." Such outbursts seem beyond Giraud's experience, and his reaction is significant: rather than kiss her invitingly upturned lips, he sticks a thermometer between them. She seems far too "hot"; but in reality it is Giraud who is far too "cold." Hence the importance of the following scene.

As it turns out, our naked neighbour was only half-nude. In fact, he

A ludicrous pantomime of ersatz passion: Lilyan Tashman and André de Beranger in *So This Is Paris*.

is a dancer in Arabian costume, naked to the waist, one Maurice Lalle by name. The film opens as Lalle and his wife rehearse their "Dance of Despair," a ludicrous pantomime of *ersatz* passion in which Maurice melodramatically "stabs" his unfaithful paramour. The acting, the gestures, are clearly overstated; and the seriousness of the scene is completely deflated when the camera pans left to the pianist who accompanies their performance. Neither dancer seems much interested in the dance, nor for that matter are they much interested in each other: hence Madame Lalle's excited reaction when Giraud walks in to protest Monsieur Lalle's nudity.

Maurice has withdrawn, and Georgette is exercising, stretching her legs, standing on her head. Indeed, she is upside down when Giraud enters, so that he is greeted by the sight of her bare legs. As it happens, those bare legs belong to an old flame. Somewhat to our surprise, we learn that Giraud and Georgette once spent "a marvellous day in the forest" together, a day on which Giraud was "particularly brilliant." Paul's surprise matches our own. He clearly enjoys the notion of illicit sex, is clearly aroused by Georgette's presence, and he gestures enthusiastically to signify his pleasure. His wife, Suzanne, in the meanwhile, has been unable to refrain from glancing at the Lalle's window, through which she now sees her husband moving his arms as if in battle. Paul senses her presence, turns around, guilt on his face, and he encourages the impression that he is locked in mortal combat. Which enables him to explain the embarrassing lack of his cane upon his eventual return home by telling Suzanne that he broke it in "three pieces" in his struggle to guarantee her integrity.

The cane, as Gerald Mast points out,[17] serves as an important but elusive metaphor, at once a social symbol (it is a gentleman's cane), a phallic symbol (Paul leaves it with Georgette, signifying his subconscious preference for extra-marital rather than marital sex), and a lie detector (to the extent that its repeated presence indicates various shifts of sexual loyalty). More important here, however, is the opportunity it provides Maurice to call upon Suzanne (he returns the cane); and the subsequent opportunity that Lalle's visit provides Suzanne for indulging her sexual fantasies. At last her sheik has arrived, all compliments and kisses, and Suzanne's conventional reaction, accepting his endearments while rejecting his advances, is indicative of her ambivalence. She had never seriously believed that her dreams would materialise; and once they are made material, she is not completely willing to accept the emotional risks implicit in dreaming.

Paul's experience is similarly instructive. Georgette has decided that Paul will prove an interesting playmate, and she lures him out of the house on several occasions, once to visit a dying "patient" (herself) and

97

The dance of desire: *Madame DuBarry* (above) and *So This Is Paris* (below).

once to attend a costume ball. Indeed, the former escapade provides opportunity for the latter. Paul is cited for speeding as he answers Georgette's call — he insults the officer who writes out the citation (Paul's insults are doubtless a show of virility in Georgette's presence) — and the eventual result is that Paul is given a three-day jail sentence, which he must begin serving the very night of the Artists' Ball.

The ball itself is significant for several reasons. First of all, it is a technical *tour-de-force* of expressionistic film-making (anticipating the carnival sequence in Murnau's *Sunrise*). The dance hall is architecturally punctuated with gigantic female legs, constructed especially for the gala event, and the leg motif dominates the kaleidoscopic montage of dancers and dancing feet. More importantly, the frenzied activity, the overwhelming expenditure of sexual energy, provides Paul the opportunity to indulge in his own saturnalian exercise. Simply by being there he comes to re-learn the thrill of sexuality (this equation of dancing with sex is essential to Lubitsch's subsequent musicals, including *That Lady in Ermine*). Indeed, Paul's sexual skills are so quickly honed that he and Georgette win the Charleston contest; and it is this victory which proves to be the film's sexual turning point.

Suzanne has remained at home, thinking her husband has gone off to jail. Lalle comes by, again with the cane, but their tryst is interrupted by the entrance of a Police Inspector. Suzanne wishes to avoid any sort of scandal, and she convinces Lalle (by elbowing him in the side and kicking him in the shins) to play the role of Doctor Giraud. Lalle co-operates — as Dr. Giraud he is allowed the pleasure of a lengthy, passionate farewell — and he goes off to serve Paul's prison term. Suzanne is understandably puzzled — where is Paul if he is not in custody? — but her puzzle is solved when the winners of the dance contest are announced over the radio: Paul is at the Artists' Ball. Clearly Suzanne would never have known of Paul's whereabouts or activities had he and Georgette not won the dance contest; thus their winning it forces Suzanne to take really aggressive action. Reading about love is not enough: Suzanne has to get actively involved, and she gets involved by dressing herself in her most alluring gown and following Paul to the "Bal des Artistes."

Paul's victory thus allows Suzanne greater knowledge of her husband. Similarly, the victory, and the bottles of champagne which accompany it, allows Paul greater knowledge of his dancing partner, Georgette, and of himself as well. Under the champagne's benign influence, Paul does not become upset when Georgette dumps him for someone else; he rather enjoys the freedom to flirt with anyone he chooses, even a cute though masked brunette who looks very much like Suzanne. Indeed, Paul gives her a big wink, and she responds by leading him to a taxi.

Betty Grable and Douglas Fairbanks, Jr. in *That Lady in Ermine*.

Together at last: the breakfast scene in *So This Is Paris*.

The film's outcome, from this point forward, is equally humorous, predictable, and appropriate. Paul goes home with his new-found paramour — who is, it turns out, his wife — and Suzanne takes home her new-found lover — who is, it turns out, her husband. To a certain degree, then, they are back where they started, husband and wife. They never untangle their respective intrigues and deceptions. If anything, Suzanne gains something of an upper hand, declaring herself henceforth to be boss at home. But, as the epilogue makes clear, something important has happened, a real change has occurred. Paul and Suzanne come to breakfast, arm in arm. They sit down at the table, Paul moves his place-setting closer to that of his wife, and the film concludes with a genuinely passionate embrace.

Miriam Hopkins "jazzes up" her marriage to *The Smiling Lieutenant* (Maurice Chevalier).

The point, which Lubitsch returns to with some frequency (c.f., *The Smiling Lieutenant, Bluebeard's Eighth Wife, That Uncertain Feeling*), is that sexual relationships cannot be taken for granted. They require effort, concern, a certain degree of risk, an occasional dash of prurience, to keep the mystery of love alive. *So This Is Paris, The Smiling Lieutenant,* and *That Uncertain Feeling,* for example, all deal with some variety of impotence or failure, and in each the solution involves a self-conscious though careful indulgence of sexual appetites. In *So This Is Paris,* then, Paul and Suzanne have the opportunity to enact their fantasies to a degree, thus to bring those fantasies usefully within the context of their marriage. In *The Smiling Lieutenant,* Ann (Miriam Hopkins) is advised to "jazz up" her *lingèrie* if she wishes to arouse her husband (Chevalier); and in *That Uncertain Feeling,* Larry (Melvyn Douglas) and Jill (Merle Oberon) are forced to go through the motions of divorce, complete with co-respondents, in order to recognise the value and significance of their marriage. Indeed, the sexual cynicism evident in such early films as *The Marriage Circle* seems clearly inoperative in Lubitsch's post-depression work. To some extent,

Nicole (Claudette Colbert) ponders her scheme to bring Bluebeard to his senses in *Bluebeard's Eighth Wife.*

Lubitsch became less daring, more conventional, in his approach to marriage as time went by (c.f., the comparison of *The Marriage Circle* and *The Shop Around the Corner*). More accurately, Lubitsch came increasingly to value the emotional integrity of sexual relationships, and those relationships, while occasionally non-marital, as in *Design for Living* and *Trouble in Paradise,* are generally conventional, as in *So This Is Paris.* Even *Bluebeard's Eighth Wife* (scripted by Billy Wilder and Charles Brackett) argues the importance of marriage. Indeed, the eighth wife (Claudette Colbert) takes her marriage so seriously that she drives her husband to a sanitorium as a means of insuring the sanity of their marriage. Marriage can be a trap (e.g., *The Student Prince, Design for Living*) but in general it is seen as the most appropriate context for personal and social well-being.

* * *

If *So This Is Paris* is concerned to equalise sexual energy and to overcome sexual inhibitions within marriage, then *The Love Parade,* like most of the Chevalier and/or MacDonald musicals which followed, is concerned, firstly, with establishing the fact of marriage, and secondly, with equalising emotional prerogatives within it: hence the frequent equation of government (Jeanette MacDonald is a queen in *Love Parade* and she effectively owns the kingdom in *The Merry Widow*) and sacrament (all of the musicals involve marriage at one point or another). *The Love Parade* thus reverses, at least in terms of its initial situation, the movement of *So This Is Paris.* In the latter film, it is the wife whose sexual needs are not being met, and it is the husband who demonstrates insufficient libido. In *The Love Parade,* on the other hand, we have a sexually reluctant (though not dispassionate) woman, Queen Louise I of Sylvania, whose reluctance is overcome by a profligate though perfectly charming philanderer, Count Renard, the first of Chevalier's several great Parisian lovers.

Renard's sexual *savoir faire* is established in the opening sequence. After Renard's servant, Jacques (Lupino Lane), sets the table for an intimate dinner (like the dinner which opens *Trouble in Paradise*), we hear the diners quarrelling behind closed doors. Eventually Renard enters, tells us that the lady within is "terribly jealous," and then the lady enters to present evidence for her case: a garter. Renard tries to laugh it off ("c'est à toi"), but the lady raises her skirts to prove that the garter is not hers. Renard hardly has time to make an excuse, however, as the lady, in her despair, takes a pistol out of her purse. The woman and the count struggle for the weapon — at which point the lady's husband enters. The woman, her integrity now compromised, turns the gun on herself and shoots herself (quite melodramatically) in the breast. The husband, in his stone-faced sorrow, picks up the weapon and, accompanied by heavy-handed violins, "shoots" Chevalier, who gamefully checks his torso for wounds before helping the husband check to see whether or not the gun was loaded (blanks). Both men look towards the woman, who looks up at them nonchalantly (in close-up), as if bored with the familiarity of it all. The husband rushes to his wife's side while Chevalier deposits the pistol in a dresser drawer, a drawer literally full of dainty, purse-sized pistols.

Without labouring the point, it is clear that sexual relationships in the Parisian world of Count Renard, as in the Viennese world of Mizzi Stock in *The Marriage Circle,* are characterised by game-playing (the "game" of suicide) and ritual (the ceremony of candlelight dinners). There is little sense of urgency in it all – the Parisians seem to find the game invigorating, as we discover when Renard sings his "Paris, Please Stay the Same" number: all of the ladies in the neighbourhood raise their glasses in salute to Renard's gamesmanship. Indeed, the only person who really takes it all seriously is the Sylvanian ambassador, whose outrage with his military attaché's "shameless escapades" is less a function of official displeasure than personal jealousy. As he tells Renard, his wife has told him everything. Accordingly, he orders Renard home to Sylvania to face the queen's wrath.

In Sylvania, on the other hand, we find a different sort of ceremony, a ceremony not of jaded sexual reality, but of frustrated sexual fantasy. We first see Queen Louise I (Jeanette MacDonald) in bed, wearing an elegant, sensual negligee, as her ladies in waiting enter her bedchamber to begin their morning offices. They bid her good morning, and the queen wonders aloud: "Why am I always awakened from my dreams?" There is no question what sort of dream she has been dreaming here. Not only does she admit it was a "wonderful" dream, but she sighs, moans, caresses herself, and hugs a pillow as if to recapture the sensual warmth of the vision. The head chambermaid then expresses the hope that the queen's dream will come true, and Louise replies: "No, I'm afraid it will always have to remain a dream."

The scenes which follow, the queen's bath, her morning meeting with her ministers, likewise centre on the issue of the queen's sexuality. All anyone ever talks of is marriage, as the queen repeatedly complains ("marriage, marriage, that's all I hear, morning and night"), and her reason for not marrying becomes clear, to us if not to herself or her subjects. Briefly, as her "Dream Lover" song indicates ("There's a land of charm that I know/Land of sweet romance where I long to go"), the queen is caught up in a vision of sexual perfection ("dream lover put

"Why am I always awakened from my dreams?"—Jeanette MacDonald as Louise I of Sylvania in *The Love Parade*.

your arms around me") so strong that sexual reality seems a sorry second. Furthermore, she is a queen, and therefore accustomed to getting her every wish. Thus her reluctance to settle for any of the suitors suggested by her ministers and her fascination with Count

Renard. Indeed, she reads the "Confidential Report" on Renard's amorous activities with the same relish that Madame Giraud in *So This Is Paris* reads her Arabian Nights fiction. The similarity between the two women is further underlined when Queen Louise suggests that the count grow a beard as penance for his frivolity. As the queen tells Renard: "That will stop your philandering — you'll have to be serious in a beard." Renard replies: "I look terrible in a beard . . . dreadful. Of course, there are men who look fine in beards, like sheiks . . . . " And Louise interjects: "Why yes, that's what I thought." Like Madame Giraud, then, Louise longs for a mythical desert prince. But unlike Madame Giraud, Louise does not have a husband on whom to bestow her overactive attentions. Furthermore, her devotion to the ideal makes her reluctant to accomodate herself to reality.

Luckily for her and for Sylvania, however, Renard makes his timely entrance and Louise's dream of sexual perfection seems fulfilled: her desert prince has arrived. And likewise Renard has a dream fulfilled. Of course, he would rather dine with the queen than suffer her wrath. But he does seem genuinely attracted to her. She is, Lubitsch makes clear, an extremely attractive and alluring woman; as we see when she gets out of bed clad only in a flimsy negligee, as we see when she takes her bath, as we see when she lifts her skirts to prove to her cabinet that her person is as attractive as her position ("my legs are perfect"). Indeed, it is this sort of charm and beauty that Renard celebrates in his "Love Parade" number ("Lips of Lucille/Beauty of Camille/ You are my ideal/ My Love Parade").

More important than the physical attraction between the two, however, is the existence of a certain emotional *camaraderie*. Both Louise and Renard are dreamers of one sort or another; furthermore, both are used to enjoying complete control over their lives. Louise reigns over Sylvania, and Renard "reigns" as the crown-prince of Parisian lovers. It is this sort of self-control which makes them interesting, which makes each something of a challenge to the other, and which allows them to sing such marvellous duets, "Anything to Please the Queen," and "Love Parade." Indeed, singing harmony requires greater self-control than singing alone, and it is the twin issues of marital harmony and marital control which the film focuses on once the marriage between Louise and Renard is solemnised.

Even before the wedding ceremony it is clear that ideals will be frustrated, that someone's prerogatives will have to suffer. As the prime minister tells us, Renard can never be king, only prince-consort. "And after all, what is a prince-consort? He's a gentleman with a thousand duties and no rights. He has nothing to say, nothing to do." Of course, Renard has one thing to do — to service the queen's sexual needs — but

107

"You are my ideal, my Love Parade."

as Renard finds out, that is hardly enough to make life interesting: he
eventually tells Louise, "I'm tired of being treated as if I were a sort of
plaything." The conventional tables are thus turned. The husband must
promise to love, cherish, and obey; the husband plays bridge and takes
tea; the husband must content himself to shop for new uniforms, etc.,

etc., while the wife is out reviewing the troops. As the Afghan Ambassador tells us, "No Chungo."

The film thus calls into question conventional marital relationships, and it does so by the device of parody. The marriage of Louise and Renard reverses and thus parodies traditional husband/wife roles. Besides, there is the sub-plot of Jacques and the queen's maid (the Frenchman and the farmer's daughter) which further serves to undercut upper-class courtship rituals. Indeed, their stormy, slapstick relationship serves to emphasise how over-conventional royal relationships can be. As the queen's maid puts it on the wedding night: "When royalty marry, they don't quarrel like common people do — they can't afford to." Jacques emphasises the point: "That's just the trouble — they can't

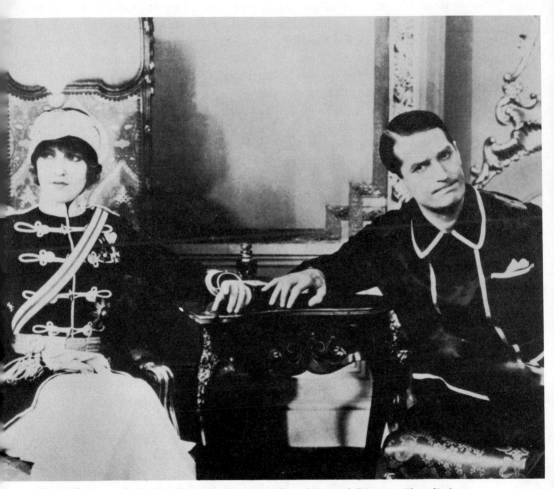

The tables turned: Louise (Jeanette MacDonald) and Renard (Maurice Chevalier) at odds in *The Love Parade*.

109

let off steam with a good old row like you or I." Thus Renard and Louise are doubly bound, by the chains of marriage and station, each reinforcing the other. The film's movement, however, is not so much to break those chains (though Renard does threaten to walk out of the marriage) as to loosen them up, to make both Louise and Renard more self-aware, more attuned to the emotional damage that chains too tightly bound can do. The point is not to attack marriage, but to humanise it, to put love and equality rather than ego and propriety at the centre.

The issue comes to a head when the queen, at her ministers' urging, commands Renard to accompany her to the opera. Renard, of course, is not at all certain that he wants to accompany Louise anywhere, much less to the opera. But it seems no longer to be a matter of personal preference. Any show of disharmony will result, according to the queen's advisors, in a loss of credibility and correspondingly in a loss of foreign credit. Either Renard goes to the opera, "in full gala uniform, all medals and decoration, and in the very best of humour," as the queen commands it, or the country goes "broke." Such a dichotomy, between personal disposition and public responsibility, is not always avoidable in Lubitsch (e.g., *The Student Prince*). But in *Love Parade,* as in *The Merry Widow,* it is clearly a false dichotomy enforced by over-rigid conventions. Renard does not have to go smilingly to the opera, nor does the country need to go broke. Indeed, Renard has become something of a fiscal expert in his long hours of enforced leisure, and he has effectively balanced the royal budget, right down to the bill for the royal dressmaker. There is no need, then, for foreign credit, and therefore there is no need for Renard's presence at the opera. But the queen and her ministers are too set in their bungling ways to consider Renard's proposal. As the prime minister puts it: "I am not permitted to receive suggestions in the affairs of state from the prince-consort." To which Renard replies, half incredulously, half knowingly, "Not even when they are good?"

Convention thus once again threatens disaster, for the royal treasury as well as the royal marriage. However, in neither case is convention itself the villain: it is rather an over-reliance on convention as it allows self-indulgence that the film is concerned to discredit. Hence it is significant that Renard does not reject convention altogether. To the contrary, the film's issues are resolved when Renard employs convention in the service of self-awareness. The Queen in her anger has gone unaccompanied to the opera, and by so doing she places herself in a public position where all show of disharmony must be avoided no matter what the cost. Renard then appears, in full uniform, to the applause of the crowd. Louise attempts to get the first word in – "As for myself, you needn't have come at all" — but Renard calls her bluff: "All right, goodbye." She grabs him by the arm, and he insists that she "beg" him to stay, one person to another, no more commands. Renard is clearly calling the shots here, and he orchestrates the play of emotion as skillfully as the conductor leads the opera-house orchestra. In both cases it is a matter of positive convention. Renard forces Louise to experience the gap between personal emotion (anger/jealousy) and public facade ("the very best of humour"): "You are a queen — you must behave." The effect, as the last scene makes clear, is that Louise learns to appreciate the emotional freedom and the emotional responsibility that such awareness allows and requires.

It is important to our understanding of the film's conclusion that Lubitsch does not question the necessity for rulers: someone has to exercise the royal prerogatives. Indeed, to exercise them is not only necessary but dangerous, as Louise demonstrates in *The Love Parade*, as Karl Heinrich demonstrates in *The Student Prince*. Without this knowledge the film's final scene might very well appear to re-assert a mindless sort of marital convention. On the surface, at least, it seems that Louise capitulates unconditionally to Renard: she would rather give up dominion than give up her husband, and she voluntarily suggests that Renard "take command, not only of the affairs of state, not only in the Department of the Navy, but also here at home."

But this conventionality is undercut and made more acceptable by two factors. First of all, the "punishment" scene is a self-conscious parody of the first meeting between Louise and Renard, right down to the details of dialogue and camera set-up. In the first scene Louise "punishes" Renard by commanding him to dine with her; and in the second scene Renard "punishes" Louise by acceding to her sexually-loaded wishes — and in neither case is the punishment anything but pleasurable. Indeed, in both cases the "punishment" is suggested by the person to be punished ("If I were in your place I'd say . . ."), and in both cases the "suggestion" is the same ("you shall stay here . . . attached to me") with one significant difference. In the first scene Renard suggests "from morning to night" as an appropriate period of attachment; and from morning to night, once they are married, he does nothing but await the Queen's return. Louise, on the other hand, begins to repeat Renard's line, but she catches herself and rephrases it — "from night till morning" — thus placing real sexuality in its proper perspective. Renard and Louise are therefore lovers in fact, not in fancy, and there is no sense that such a love will require either partner to be merely a "plaything."

Secondly, even if Renard were to "take command," as Louise quite mockingly suggests, it seems inconceivable that he would exercise

The Colonel (Douglas Fairbanks) ponders his situation beneath the portrait of *That Lady in Ermine* (Betty Grable).

command unwisely or so as to humiliate Louise. After all, he has literally played the "wife" role, both sexually and socially, and there can be little doubt that Renard would not only allow but insist that Louise take an active part in the governing process. To begin with, Renard admires active, self-assertive women, and he knows full well how stifling inactivity can be. Furthermore, governing Sylvania is not necessarily to be seen as a pleasant chore. Louise can hardly be said to enjoy her morning cabinet meetings, and the demands of protocol do not always accord with emotional inclination. Indeed, rulers in Lubitsch are generally a put-upon lot, reigning over insignificant kingdoms with the help of incompetent ministers, and it is only when such responsibility is shared that social concord of any sort can be maintained. Such is the case in *The Merry Widow* (King Achmed consults Queen Dolores on the issue of appointing a special envoy to bring the merry widow home), in *That Lady in Ermine* (the marriage of Angelina and the Count reconciles Bergamo and Hungary), and such is clearly the case in *The Love Parade*. Indeed, all of these films hold out for emotional equality within the context of humane societies and conventions; and the notion of a "love parade," an organised ritual celebrating emotional integrity, seems perfectly to symbolise the humanistic Lubitsch vision of life and love's place in it.

* * *

In *Ninotchka,* as in his other films, Lubitsch sets up several interlocking symbol systems signifying or embodying personal/social choices. One such system is a function of "place." In *Design for Living,* for example, emotional issues are represented by the contrasts of Paris versus London, Paris versus Utica, Montmartre versus the business district, and so on. In *Ninotchka* Lubitsch employs a similar "place" scheme to embody thematic issues. Where is Ninotchka's proper place in life: Paris or Petrograd? Moscow or Constantinople? The answer for Garbo's Ninotchka, clearly, is the latter. She can be a good Russian in Constantinople, a place equidistant from both Moscow and Paris, a place where she can be equally loyal to herself, to Leon (Melvyn Douglas), and to her people.

Another such scheme, ultimately more important for Lubitsch, represents emotional issues by a paradigm of character types and attitudes. Lubitsch thus constructs a compassionate sort of comic dialectic in which options are personified and choices are made. In *Lady Windermere's Fan,* for example, Mrs. Erlynne must choose between Lord Lorton, who represents financial and social security, and

113

Divorce 1940-style: Sebastion (Burgess Meredith), Larry (Melvyn Douglas), and Jill (Merle Oberon) in *That Uncertain Feeling*.

her daughter, who represents, at the moment of Mrs. Erlynne's choosing, social and emotional insecurity. That is, Lady Windermere is unsure of Lord Windermere's affections, and Mrs. Erlynne risks insecurity to go to her daughter's rescue. Or in *That Uncertain Feeling*, to take a second example, Jill (Merle Oberon) must choose either the *avant-garde* eccentricity of the misanthropic Sebastian (Burgess Meredith) or the emotional stability of her newly self-aware husband (Melvyn Douglas).

To be sure, this sort of organisational scheme, assigning a range of characters to represent a range of motives and feelings, is typical not only of Lubitsch, but it is an implicit part of stage and screen dramaturgy in general. What matters, however, and what distinguishes one artist from the next, is the particular set of issues that such character schemes raise and resolve; by now it should be clear that there is a consistency of humane concern across the Lubitsch canon.

Let us consider, then, the range of characters and choices in *Ninotchka*. At one extreme of the character scale is the White Russian Grand Duchess Swana (Ina Claire), a woman of grace, elegance, and apparent wealth, who is, however, selling her memoirs to the magazines. As Leon puts it to her: "We won't have to bother about our future if you are willing to raffle off your past." Swana seems to combine qualities of Madame Colet, the widow Sonia, and Mrs. Matuschek. She is simultaneously stylish, bored, and desperate; and the choice that life offers her is a sad one. She can either fight to keep her noblewoman's jewelery from falling into the hands of Soviet agents (Ninotchka and the boys), a fight she will surely lose. Or she can give up the jewels in order to keep her lover, the Count Leon d'Algout. But Leon, once he has met Ninotchka, is a lover who will not be kept against his will; so once again Swana can only suffer. She has already lost her palace in Petrograd, her tsar, her country, and her people, as she tells Ninotchka; she has lost, in other words, her culture, a culture that she struggles in a pitiable expatriate fashion to maintain. And she lost her culture because she did not love it deeply enough. Russia, for her, was a life of elegant, irrelevant ruling-class ceremony, all jewels and surface glitter. Even in exile Swana maintains this sort of superficial stance. When we first see her she complains that her "face doesn't compose well . . . all highlights." This concern for surfaces accounts for her callous disregard of the lower strata of society. She may fuss over her face, and buy sweaters for her dog, but she apparently had no qualms whatsoever about loosing the Cossacks on the serfs. Thus her love of Russia, as Ninotchka points out, was not of the sort that inspires love in return.

There is, however, something to be said in Swana's defence. First of all, she is self-aware though cynical. As she says to Leon, "I guess one gets the face one deserves." Furthermore, her comment to Ninotchka that the Cossacks should have used guns rather than whips is motivated less by hatred of the Russian people than by jealousy. Even in her bitterness she does not really seem to be sadistic; and her jealousy, in turn, indicates a murky, almost tragic awareness on her part that she is about to lose the last love of her life. Leon and her jewels represent the last emotional links with her past, with her youth; and those links, once severed by time and history, can never be repaired. Thus we are led to pity Swana at the same time as we are forced to reject her.

The other extreme of the character scale is represented by the often-mentioned but seldom seen Stalinist commissar Razinin, played, appropriately enough, by Bela Lugosi. Razinin in his Draconian

115

The Duchess (Ina Claire) makes an offer: she will hand over the jewels if Ninotchka will leave Paris and Leon forever.

blood-thirstiness is the Red Russian equivalent of Swana's White Russian Cossacks: he is far too eager (as report has it) to send subordinates off to Siberia. Thus, like Swana herself, Razinin reveals too little love of the Russian people. He is more concerned with maintaining a paranoid orthodoxy of ideals and an oddly bourgeois sense of diplomatic dignity. Razinin reigns over his soulless bureaucracy much as the tsar reigned over a soulless monarchy. And neither sort of tyranny inspires love or loyalty.

At the film's beginning, then, Ninotchka sees her choices only in red and white. From the very first moment we see her, standing almost

116

On the verge of laughter: Ninotchka (Garbo) and Leon (Melvyn Douglas) share a table in a worker's cafe.

defiantly alone on the railway platform, she spouts the strict party line in every matter. She even agrees with Razinin's bloodthirsty methods, and praises the most recent mass trials for creating "fewer but better Russians." But we do not really doubt Ninotchka's motives. She is completely and admirably sincere when she upbraids Iranoff, Buljanoff, and Kopalski for giving half of every much needed loaf to the enemy. She does love the Russian people, and her love is a matter of direct experience. As she tells Leon, she grew up on a farm, fought as a sergeant in the army, and hence the Russian people are not, for her, a convenient ideological abstraction but a meaningful human reality.

The difficulty, of course, is that ideologies always tend towards the abstract and the inhuman. The fact that Ninotchka manages to inject a sincere measure of humane concern into an otherwise self-importantly rigid and oppressive system speaks to her credit. But Ninotchka also lets the system squelch her own humanity. In order to serve the state Ninotchka must repress her sexuality and frivolity. She must give up laughing and loving; and as far as Lubitsch is concerned that is a high (though sometimes necessary) price to pay, and particularly high when paid in the service of a ruthless and soulless state.

What Lubitsch holds out for, then, is a party neither of reds nor whites but of laughers and lovers. Hence the importance and the necessity of Count Leon d'Algout, the man Ninotchka falls in love with, the man who teaches her to laugh. But putting it that way, as if Ninotchka were a poor little commie who just needed a good man to set her straight, is to misrepresent the nature of the Leon/Ninotchka relationship. Like many Lubitsch lovers before them, Leon and Ninotchka are equals in wit and spirit. So that while Leon teaches Ninotchka to be a woman, Ninotchka in turn teaches Leon to be a man of integrity and concern, the sort of man that a woman like her can genuinely love.

If the trouble with Ninotchka is that she takes herself too seriously, the trouble with Leon is that he does not take himself seriously enough. He is something of a gigolo at first, a man who serves Swana not for love of Swana but for love of platinum watches with diamond numbers. He becomes her well-tailored Boy Friday because elegance and style mean more to him than self-respect. To be sure, he is, after his own fashion, perfectly happy to exploit and be exploited, to be a gigolo, to be a professional dandy; in part, it is his dandyness which makes him attractive, both to us and to Ninotchka. As she puts it, his "general appearance is not distasteful." He is suave, self-confident, and opportunistic; and what he needs is not to give up his romantic gestures but the opportunity to replace his cynicism with the romantic substance that will give those gestures meaning. He needs the opportunity, in other words, to fall in love without thinking that love is "juvenile and rather middle-class."

So Leon represents a kind of capitalist cynicism which allows him to exploit and be exploited. He meets Ninotchka, a woman who is not adept at playing cynical games, and Leon, to his credit, begins to question his own cynicism. As Swana tells us, Leon undergoes a sort of "regeneration" — given the choice between Swana and Ninotchka, he rightly chooses love over exploitation, and will travel the world in order to find his proper "place," beside the woman he loves.

Ninotchka undergoes a similar sort of comic death and rebirth. Like Danilo in *The Merry Widow,* Ninotchka is a special envoy whose mission is to retrieve a national treasure. Also like Danilo, Ninotchka gets sidetracked by love and fermented beverage. Thus she is literally "stood up against the wall" as comic punishment for her transgressions.

The shot, however, is not a rifle report but the joyful pop of a champagne cork, and it is not Ninotchka that is killed so much as her totally unjustified sense of guilt. She thinks herself a traitor simply because she has danced, laughed, and fallen in love ("No one can be so happy without being punished"). Lubitsch's point, however, is that people should not feel guilty for claiming their inalienable rights as human beings. Ninotchka is not asked to give up her politics. She remains a dedicated Marxist-Leninist, rightly proud of the positive accomplishments of the revolution. But she becomes a more humane Marxist-Leninist, one who can cook a collective omelette and sing songs with good friends without feeling the pangs of unnecessary guilt.

If, therefore, Lubitsch is not condemning socialism *per se* but rather the abuses of socialism which deny human beings the rights to love and laughter, what then are we to make of the film's conclusion? What sense does it make for Ninotchka to leave Russia forever? Does the film's ending do full duty to the still unresolved political opposition between capitalism and communism?

I, for one, do not think it does. The very private and romantic conclusion, Ninotchka and Leon embracing on that exotic Near Eastern balcony, does not resolve, in any meaningful fashion, the political issues. It expresses instead Lubitsch's sense of priorities. Lovers come first in the Lubitsch universe, even when love is doomed (e.g., *The Student Prince*) or unconventional (e.g. *Design for Living*) and accordingly Lubitsch settles the personal issues (issues, I might add, which can be settled) before considering the political problems. The difficulty, of course, is that the political issues in the film are insoluble. The film was made, after all, in 1939, a point in history when it was clear to many that European civilization was in danger of extinction (recall the Nazis on the railway platform on the day of Ninotchka's arrival in Paris). There simply was not world enough and time to carry on ideological arguments. As Ninotchka tells us in her pixilated soliloquy: "Bombs will fall . . . all civilization will crumble." And the most a person can ask is that destruction be delayed. As Ninotchka so touchingly, so transcendently puts it: "Not yet, please . . . wait, wait . . . what's the hurry? Let us be happy . . . give us our moment." This is precisely what Lubitsch does: he gives Leon and Ninotchka their private moment of happiness, the happiness rightly due to lovers who make proper choices, who love fully and unselfishly; and he leaves the world and its political madness to take care of itself.

Thus *Ninotchka* is not, as John Baxter describes it, "a hard, brightly-lit, cynical comedy with the wise crack completely in control."[18] It is a film by turns romantic and sceptical in the deepest sense of both words. As always with Lubitsch, compassion is the key,

Their magic moment: Garbo and Douglas in *Ninotchka*.

compassion for those who are bound to fail, like Swana, and for those who have the comic vitality to succeed, however briefly, at being warm and gentle and loving, like Ninotchka and Leon. Thus compassion is always the right stance to take, the right choice to make, particularly in the face of a self-destructive political reality. Hence Ninotchka's proper place in life is in the arms of the man she loves; for it is only by getting the lovers together, whether they be snails, birds, or people, that any sort of viable society can hope to rise from the political ashes. Thus the lovers of the world may hope to unite after the holocaust has passed. By so uniting, the tension between personal needs and social responsibility will be resolved in a personalist society where individual needs and social needs are inseparable, where it won't be the raised arm, or the raised fist, but the kiss that symbolises human aspiration.

5   Age Shall Not Wither: *Heaven Can Wait* (1943) and *Cluny Brown* (1946)

On the surface, at least, *Heaven Can Wait* represents the Lubitsch contribution to the "cinema of memory" that came of age in the early and middle Forties. Films such as *Citizen Kane* (1941), *How Green Was My Valley* (1941), *The Magnificent Ambersons* (1942), and *It's a Wonderful Life* (1946) often shared common concerns, attitudes, and narrative devices. Both *Kane* and *How Green Was My Valley,* for example, are narrated in flashback: and in both cases the flashback structure allows the film-maker to reflect upon the value of past experience. All four films, furthermore, characterise the past as a sequence of decay *(Ambersons, How Green)* and/or frustration *(Kane, Wonderful Life).* That is, the child-like innocence of the past is often portrayed as strongly attractive but insufficiently realistic: one cannot remain child-like forever. It is Kane's childish assertion of the unfettered will, for example, that eventually brings about his emotional and physical destruction. Nevertheless, past innocence is not to be rejected, but should rather be valued in memory as a matter of once enacted and still vital principles. Thus Huw Morgan ties up his family bible and his miner's boots in his mother's shawl as he prepares to leave his once green but now coal-blackened valley forever. In leaving, Huw does not turn his back on the past; he simply recognises that the past leads inevitably through the present into the future; and the future, particularly for a Catholic like Ford, can only be understood in terms of a timeless spiritual reality: the world cannot redeem itself. On the

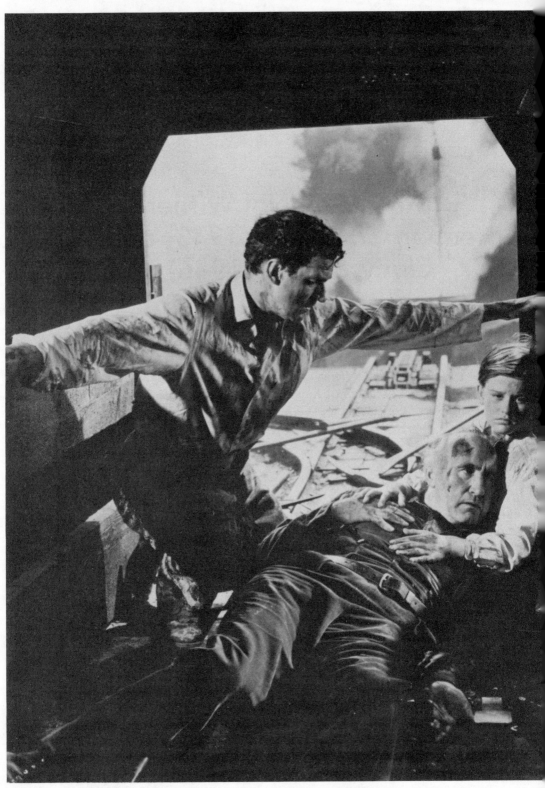

Walter Pidgeon, Donald Crisp, and Roddy McDowall in John Ford's *How Green was My Valley*.

contrary, life in a fallen world can only continue its pattern of physical and spiritual decay.

Heaven Can Wait employs a similar flashback structure. The film begins at a point in time after the death of the main character; and the film narrative represents Henry Van Cleve's "life story" as Henry (Don Ameche) tells that story to Satan. Yet Lubitsch employs that structure, not to reinforce a Wellesian sense of fatalism, but specifically to reject it. In other words, Lubitsch asserts quite clearly that Henry Van Cleve's guilt feelings are very little justified by the life he led. He may have been sexually adventurous, socially unconventional, emotionally unrestrained — he may even have told lies on occasion, but he was never genuinely immoral; his transgressions, such as they were, always retained a certain child-like purity; and his vitality is always portrayed as a positive force within the social matrix.

The film's central issue, at least as Henry perceives it, concerns this conflict of sexual energy and social propriety. Even Hell itself is a very proper place. Satan wears an impeccably-tailored cutaway coat, and he sports a precisely-trimmed Van Dyke beard. Henry too is dressed for the occasion, in mourning black; and he applies for admittance to hell as if he were applying for acceptance to Harvard. He addresses Satan as "Your Excellency" — and he seems almost comfortable with the ritualistic formality of the interview. One gets the impression, indeed, that Henry has an emotional investment in the codes of social conduct. At heart, Henry rather enjoys the exhilaration of breaking the rules: he would have been lost without rules to break.

But Henry does not go around breaking rules indiscriminately. On the contrary, Henry's sins are almost entirely a matter of sexual impropriety. The only other soul he meets in hell is an old flame; and when Henry sets about to catalogue his transgressions he does so in terms of his relationships with members of the opposite sex. As Henry puts it to Satan: "Perhaps the best way to tell you the story of my life is to tell you about the women in my life." From the very beginning Henry equates sex with guilt: he describes his mother, for example, as "a lovely lady, but prejudiced. She thought I was wonderful — she was the first woman I ever fooled." Already, then, Henry reveals an unjustified sense of personal inadequacy — which proves ultimately to be the motive force behind Henry's rather harmless philandering. That is, Henry is encouraged by his family and by the society in general to take his completely healthy instincts as evidence of moral culpability. Indeed, his family exacerbates the situation by attempting to deny Henry the prerogatives of growing up. They seek to monopolise his affections (everyone spoils him, to the point of suffocation) and to dominate his future (his father already has him slated for Harvard). As

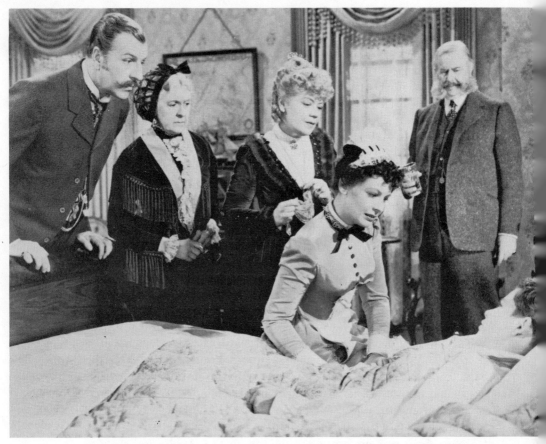

The Van Cleve clan and the french maid: Louis Calhern, Clara Blandick, Spring Byington, Signe Hasso, Charles Coburn, and Dickie Moore in *Heaven Can Wait*.

young Henry describes the situation to the fashionable french maid: "it's a conspiracy to keep me in short pants — they think they own me body and soul." The maid summarises the situation in sympathetic and appropriately sexual terms: "your soul is bigger than your pants." Henry therefore believes himself to be sexually flawed; and as a youth he seeks that one special girl who will both complement and transform him, a girl who will accomodate his sexuality in terms that the society will accept and who will do so without requiring Henry to abandon his instinctual, enthusiastic life-style.

Henry's vitality is therefore doubly threatened. On the one hand there is the slight possibility that he will become a stuffed-shirt like his cousin Albert, "the pride of all the Van Cleves." Albert was, Henry goes on to tell us, "the fulfillment of a parent's dream: always the highest in his class, never had he thrown a stone into a window, nor did he ever put a mouse in his teacher's bustle." Such a transformation is highly unlikely, though, however earnestly Henry's parents might desire it. Henry is clearly Henry, a devil-may-care young dandy; and Albert, likewise, is clearly Albert, all business and wire-rim glasses; and never the twain shall meet. On the other hand, however, there is the very real probability that Henry will dissipate his energies, sexual and otherwise, in an endless search for the perfect mate. Carried to the extreme, such a quest is sterility in action. If fathering the next generation is left entirely to men like Albert, then the resulting society will be deadeningly humourless. Indeed, Albert's notion of a high time is a visit to Grant's tomb.

The issue comes to a head on Henry's twenty-sixth birthday. To begin with, Henry has been out all night with a "musical comedy girl," or so his parents think. They are very upset with their son ("at least

Heaven Can Wait: Albert introduces the Strabels—(left to right) Eugene Pallette, Gene Tierney, Marjorie Main, and Allen Joslyn.

poor grandmother, may her soul rest in peace, was spared seeing a day like this"); and cousin Albert is equally distraught. He has chosen the occasion of Henry's birthday to introduce his *fiancée* and her Kansas City parents to the Van Cleve clan, and he fears the embarrassment that Henry's absence would engender: "As a Van Cleve I have a right to demand that he keep the shadow of scandal off the family name." But it has not been scandalous behaviour (at least not in Albert's sense of the word "scandal") that has kept Henry out all night. On the contrary, Henry had intended to raise cain, but he could not do it. He rather spent the evening riding around in a cab doing his best to forget a girl that he had met that afternoon. It was not a matter of Henry's disliking the girl, however. If anything, his malaise indicates the degree of his frustration. She is a "most beautiful princess"; and the thought of her prompts Henry to ask his mother: "when you saw father for the first time, did you feel that unmistakable something? Did you feel an electric spark from your head right down to your toes?" Her reply ("Heaven forbid") indicates the general energy level of the Van Cleve family; but the fact that Henry asks indicates the drift of his own inclination.[19] Unfortunately, he does not know who the girl is or where she lives: hence his desire to forget her. He understands, as we understand, that fixation on the unattainable is self-destructive. Mrs. Van Cleve, however, interprets Henry's mention of marriage in the general case: "Another girl will come along; I'll look for one myself . . . . And when I find a girl for you, she'll be Miss Right; and do you know where we'll find her? In the home of Mr. and Mrs. Right." We forgive Mrs. Van Cleve her concern with family propriety here: she waxes genuinely rapturous over the possibility that Henry will finally settle down. But it is clear that Henry's romantic desires are beyond his mother's understanding.

The issue is further complicated later that evening when Henry comes downstairs to meet Albert's *fiancée*. "Cousin Martha," it turns out, is the fairy princess of the day before: and the painful expression on both their faces when Albert introduces them indicates the frustration in store for both should the intended marriage between Martha and Albert take place. Again, we see the conflict of romantic longings and social pressures. Lubitsch gives us reaction-shot close-ups of Henry and Martha as they recognise each other. But most of the scene is filmed in three-shot, Henry in profile screen left, Albert facing us in the middle, Martha in profile screen right. There is a stiff formality to the shot, reflecting the social necessities of the situation, yet there is a union of emotion between Henry and Martha: they look straight into each other's eyes (although Martha does fiddle with the bodice of her dress and with her hankie); and Albert seems almost literally to exist in another plane, to fade into the background.

126

Martha and Henry are clearly birds of a similar romantic feather; and both find their romanticism to be at odds with parental inclination. We have already observed Henry's romanticism at work. We first see Martha's in the following scene — a flashback within a flashback — wherein Henry relates the story of their meeting the day before. We see both of them using public phones at a department store; and Martha arouses Henry's attention by lying to her mother. That is, Martha tells her mother that she is at the hairdresser's and will be delayed. Of course, as Henry points out in his narration, he would have followed this "angel" even if she had not lied to her mother. But the important points for our discussion are first that Martha has to account to her mother for every minute of her day, and secondly that Martha uses the opportunity gained by lying to go shopping for a sex manual at Brentano's book store. There is no question of Martha's basic integrity here; nor is there any question regarding the genuine propriety of her behaviour. She is self-aware enough to be concerned with sexual technique, but she is reticent enough to request a female sales-clerk. Unknown to Martha, however, Henry has followed her into the store; and as Henry observes her looking for help he quickly puts down his hat and assumes the sales-clerk role. Naturally, then, he assures Martha that he is adept at dealing with delicate matters ("they call me the book-worm's little mother") and he does his best to gain her attention (and her address) by assuring her that, were she marrying him, he would want her just as she is, "so charming, so young, and so beautiful." Henry finally gets so caught up in his poetic rapture that he breaks down and tells her the truth: "I took one look at you and followed you into the store." Martha pretends to be outraged and rushes out the door; but when a policeman asks her if Henry is annoying her, she changes her tune. She is clearly pleased by Henry's compliments and is fascinated by the ingenuity of his courtship behaviour.

Henry's romantic ingenuity is put to the test in the following scene — which returns us, chronologically, to the day of Henry's twenty-sixth birthday. Martha has been seized by a sneezing fit in the middle of Mrs. Cooper-Cooper's aria. A rather mortified Albert ushers Martha out of the room ("if it were just a relative it wouldn't be half so embarrassing") and suggests that she retire to the library in order to compose herself. Already, then, we see the opposition of natural instinct and social propriety; and the exact nature of that conflict is clarified when Martha unexpectedly encounters Henry in the library. Henry asks point blank her reason for marrying Albert. It is already clear from the conversation that she does not love Albert: indeed, she is angry with Henry for raising the issue. And when Henry pops the question ("an angel like you, and Albert?") Martha breaks down and tells the truth. It is either Albert or Kansas, as Martha reads the

127

The triumph of hope over expediency: Henry (Don Ameche) proposes to Martha (Gene Tierney).

situation. Her over-fed pioneer parents, it turns out, thrive on contrariness — when one says yes, the other says no, and vice versa — and "Albert came at one of those rare moments when they were both on speaking terms." As a woman, Martha feels bound by propriety to respect her parents' wishes (she never thinks of marrying without their consent — at least not before she meets Henry); and therefore she accepts Albert's proposal as her most likely opportunity. As she tells Henry between sobs: "I didn't want to be an old maid — not in Kansas!" Henry must therefore employ his ingenuity in the service of instinctual, emotional integrity. That is, he must offer Martha a viable alternative both to Kansas and Albert; and that alternative, naturally enough, is marriage to Henry himself. Martha protests that Henry is "mad," that she will never be able to look her father in the face, that she hasn't "got a thing" with her; but she is clearly overjoyed if bewildered when Henry picks her up and carries her away.

It is largely true that the elopement and marriage of Henry and Martha represents a triumph of hope over expediency, of natural instinct over social decorum, of romanticism over mercantilism. Certainly up to this point in the film we tend to side unquestioningly with Henry and Martha and the sort of emotional integrity which they embody. But there are several factors which mediate against a strict "either/or" reading of *Heaven Can Wait*. That is, we cannot completely reject people like Albert, people who seem at first the butts of Lubitsch's social satire; no more than we can completely admire every action that Henry or Martha take. We must remember that every incident in the film is demonstrative, in Henry's estimation, of Henry's qualification for damnation. To be sure, Lubitsch on the whole rejects Henry's overdeveloped sense of culpability; but Lubitsch does not portray Henry as the embodiment of perfection either. Indeed, the several remaining episodes serve to place Henry's minor and completely human transgressions within the larger context of time; and the gradual shift in perspective effectively humanises every character in the film.

Martha's parents, Mr. and Mrs. E. F. Strabel, for example, are clearly the most objectionable characters in Henry's life. Mr. Strabel (Eugene Pallette) is, according to Albert, "one of the great meat packers" of the era; and both of the elder Strabels seem habituated to tossing their considerable weight around. Indeed, they are so used to having their provincial way that they instantly disinherit their daughter for eloping with Henry (*Mr. Strabel:* "She'll never see another nickel of mine"). Even here, however, their motives are less a matter of inherent cruelty than hurt feelings and damaged pride. Thus, when Martha arrives at their Kansas City doorstep ten years later, they manage, through all their bluff and bluster, to bid her a tearful and loving welcome home. They are human after all — human enough to quarrel loud and long over the Sunday funnies — and Lubitsch grants them full credit for their humanity, however imperfect it may be.

Our vision of Albert undergoes a similar modification. He follows Martha to the Strabel house in the hope that the split between Henry and Martha will become permanent. He still admires her greatly, still longs to marry her, and he does his sincere if prosaic best to argue his middle-class case. He begins on a slightly self-righteous note, telling Martha that she has "paid" for her mistakes "and paid dearly." Martha gently rejects any notion of regret ("there were moments in my marriage which few women have been lucky enough to have experienced"); but Albert presses on in his completely earnest yet business-like manner to urge the prudence of marriage to a man like himself:

If I were, for instance, a suit of clothes, you wouldn't call me a stylish cut, and I prefer it that way. But I can safely say I'm made of solid material. I'm sewed together carefully. And my lining is good, Martha. Frankly, I believe I wear well. I'm not too hot in the summer, and I give protection in the winter. Need I say more?

Martha's reply ("No, Albert, you've given a complete and accurate description of yourself") manages to reject his proposal without belittling his sincerity. Albert will never be an adequate match for a woman like Martha; but he is far more self-aware than we had at first suspected. He is, however middle-class his metaphor, a human being with a human heart; and such people are always to be valued in Lubitsch.

This Kansas City episode also serves to humanise Henry and Martha, to place their otherwise marvellous vitality within a context of human frailty. Clearly something is amiss, or else Martha would not suddenly have fled New York to visit Kansas City. But the precise nature of the rupture is never fully defined. Henry, for example, seems at a genuine loss when grandfather Van Cleve (Charles Coburn) asks the reasons for Martha's departure. Martha herself, when she arrives in Kansas City, refuses "to hear a single unpleasant word about the last ten years" (just as Gilda in *Design for Living* refuses to hear Max refer to Tom and George as "hooligans"). It is only when Henry and grandfather follow Martha to Kansas City and sneak into the Strabel house (as Tom and George follow Gilda to Utica) that we are given an indication of Martha's motives.

The entire Henry/Martha confrontation scene is a masterpiece of shifting moods and multiple meanings. Henry, for example, appeals first to Martha's kind heart ("can't you imagine how I suffered?") but quickly shifts to the attack ("what's Albert doing here?") when Martha tells him that "it won't work anymore." Henry is genuinely disturbed; but he deals with his anxiety by consciously and blatantly ennacting the "wronged husband" role, hoping that his assumed martyrdom will arouse some measure of guilt or sympathy on Martha's part. Martha sees through it, of course ("Henry, I know your every mood"), and Henry understands that; but he perseveres and shifts stance once again: now he is the wrongdoer ("I know I've brought you nothing but unhappiness") seeking forgiveness. It is all a marvellously elaborate emotional dance, both verbally (as Henry and Martha spar) and visually (as Henry follows Martha around the room); and the dance is necessary for two reasons. First of all, Henry does not know which particular indiscretion on his part sent Martha packing, and he has to keep dancing lest she pin him down. Secondly, there is the fact that Martha really loves him—finds even his childish folly lovable and

130

ultimately forgivable—and the longer Henry can keep her dancing the more likely she is to come to her emotional and marital senses, which is precisely what happens, with a little help from grandfather Van Cleve.

For a moment, at least, it seems that Henry really has lost Martha'a affection. It is ten years to the day since they eloped together—and in the midst of their elaborate quarrel the clock strikes, reminding both of them that it's the twenty-fifth of October. Martha wishes Henry "many happy returns" on his birthday; and Henry, in return, points out that it is their anniversary as well. Martha is almost willing to forgive him at this point ("it is very difficult for a women to send her husband away on their tenth anniversary"); but Henry accompanies his best wishes with an anniversary present, an expensive diamond bracelet. At the sight of the bracelet Martha's demeanour changes, grows suddenly cold; and we quickly come to understand why. Martha, it turns out, had inadvertently come across a bill from Cartiers, a bill listing two purchases, two bracelets in fact, one bought in early May for $500, the other in late May for $10,000. She had received neither prior to the evening of their Kansas City confrontation, had assumed that Henry was seriously ($10,500 worth) involved with someone else, and had then decided to leave New York. She had not, however, asked for an explanation, and she is little inclined, even after Henry gives her the $10,000 present, to accept his assertion that the bill was in error. To be sure, Henry's explanation does sound rather desperate; but with the presentation of the $10,000 bracelet to Martha the gravity of the situation changes. Martha nevertheless perseveres in disbelieving; Henry continues to urge his basic innocence; and grandfather then attempts to break the emotional deadlock: "Come on, come on, sweep her off her feet." Henry protests that he does not want Martha to return unless she does so willingly. Indeed, he argues with a solemn, very straight face, that divorce is the answer, and that Martha should take their son Jackie, pleading Jackie's best interests are involved: "do you want him to grow up to be another Henry Van Cleve?"

Henry then presses his self-deprecating case in order to force Martha's hand. Young Jackie, as Henry tells the tale, has been buying ice cream for several little girls, with rather embarrassing results. "You should have seen little Jackie trying to get himself out of that situation," Henry tells Martha. Martha's maternal curiosity is aroused, and she asks after Jackie's success. Henry reports with pride that one "little girl likes him better than before"—implying that certain sorts of indiscretion can have beneficial results. Indeed, Martha inadvertently finds herself agreeing that certain transgressions are forgivable. On the subject of Jackie and his "little stories" she remarks: "He wants you to believe them so badly that you wish you could, and finally what can you do but . . ." Martha stops herself suddenly, as it dawns on her that Henry's own "little stories" are of the same sort and are equally innocent: if Jackie can be forgiven his ice cream cones, Henry should be forgiven the occasional $500 bracelet.

All of which would seem to indicate that Henry has been unable completely to renounce his stage-door past. And it indicates, further, that Martha rather prefers Henry's romantic foolishness to the eventless routine of life in the Strabel household. Like *So This Is Paris* and *That Uncertain Feeling, Heaven Can Wait* argues the necessity for a little harmless prurience if life and love are to remain interesting. As Henry puts it to Martha as they prepare to sneak out of the house: "how many people are lucky enough to have the thrill of eloping twice in one marriage?" The difficulty, however, is that marital high jinks can be carried too far in the direction of mistrust, as Martha almost demonstrates. Even had Henry been handing out $500 bracelets, Martha ought to have been forgiving, so long as Henry's loyalty remained genuinely with herself and Jackie. Furthermore, there is some possibility that Henry really has not sinned at all (which would make Martha's leaving all the more questionable). After they have agreed to elope for the second time, Henry points out the extraordinary mutuality of their relationship: "How many women love their husbands enough to forgive them and take them back and start all over again . . . and how many men love their wives enough to lie and say they're guilty when they have really done nothing wrong?" We never do discover which of Henry's "little stories" is the "lie" which he speaks of here. The point, however, is that Henry's human imperfections are, by comparison with his enthusiastic and genuine adoration of Martha, a matter of slight concern. All in all, Henry is a splendid if occasionally vainglorious fellow, and Martha knows it: hence her willingness to forgive, to forget, and to elope once again with the man she loves.

Life has, therefore, a way of repeating itself in *Heaven Can Wait,* as Henry and Martha demonstrate by eloping for a second time. This cyclical principle serves to moderate the tone of Lubitsch's satire. Early in the film, for example, we side with Henry and Martha as they struggle to break free of parental domination; and we might reasonably expect that Henry will be careful to avoid the sort of over-domineering parental behaviour that set Henry and his own parents at odds. This is not the case, however; Henry may never cease to be dashing, in a quaintly old-fashioned way, despite his spreading girth, but as time progresses, and as young Jackie matures, Henry becomes very much the "old-fashioned father," even to the extent of buying off a "follies" girl that young Jack had become involved with. As Henry puts it to Martha, in an attempt to justify his over-active concern for Jack's welfare: "It's

Eloping for the second time: Grandpa (Charles Coburn), Martha (Gene Tierney),
and Henry (Don Ameche) Van Cleve.

a father's function to save his son from the mistakes he made." Clearly
Henry's motive here is not to squelch Jack's vitality, no more than it
was Mrs. Van Cleve's motive to squelch Henry's years ago. It is simply a
natural condition of parenthood to exercise such concern, just as it is a
natural condition of youth to bridle at parental control.

Yet it is not that simple: we cannot set age against youth any more
readily than we can set Henry against Albert. Indeed, as Albert
demonstrates, young people can be just as cautious, just as proper, as
their elders. And Grandfather Van Cleve demonstrates just the
contrary, that old folks can be every bit as spry and vital as their
juniors. Lubitsch argues no clean and easy scheme of human virtue.
Albert and Henry, for example, however dissimilar their behaviour,

share a common ancestry; and there is no readily perceivable logic behind the differences in their personalities. Albert is Albert and Henry is Henry: we must accept that as a fact. But we do not therefore argue "senselessness" as a general rule in *Heaven Can Wait.* To the contrary, the difference between Albert and Henry symbolises an essential condition of existence. Henry could not be Henry without Albert's presence. The two men are contraries which we come to understand as necessary complements. Were it not for people like Albert we would have no reason to value people like Henry; while if society's continued existence were left totally to people like Henry, we no doubt would come to value the prosaic common sense of folk like Albert.

In *Heaven Can Wait,* then, Lubitsch argues for a sort of accepting, self-aware forgiveness. Thematically, this forgiveness extends in varying degrees to every character in the film. Dramatically, however, the film's theme is specified as the forgiveness accorded to Henry at the film's conclusion, when Satan rejects Henry's application for admittance to Hades ("Sorry, Mr. Van Cleve, but we don't cater to your class of people here"). Everything considered, Henry has lead a socially-fruitful existence, vital, ever-hopeful, never mean or ungenerous. Therefore, while he may not go directly to "the main building," may have to spend "a few hundred years" in the "annex," there is every reason to believe he will eventually gain admittance to Heaven's main halls. As Satan points out, Henry has friends "among the residents in the main building," people like Martha and grandfather Van Cleve who preceded Henry in death, and there can be no question that they will plead eloquently in Henry's defence. As a man gives, so shall he receive; and Henry clearly deserves the beautiful death (he dies to the strains of the "Merry Widow Waltz") and the heavenly reward which Lubitsch so mercifully, so marvellously, accords him.

* * *

Cluny Brown is clearly a marvellous film, rich with grace and feeling, a clear expression of Lubitsch's deeply felt humanity. In fact, I cannot resist comparing it in this regard to Shakespeare's *The Tempest,* for both are deeply concerned with the relationship of self and society. Both works are, to begin with, about exiles, men of intellect and principle who are banished from their homelands by dictators greedy for wealth and power. Also, in both *Cluny Brown* and *The Tempest* we see a young girl of wit and enthusiasm who finds a lover and, along with him, a brave new world (although in *Cluny Brown* the exile and the lover are one and the same).

More importantly, both *The Tempest* and *Cluny Brown* have a strong

Cluny Brown (Jennifer Jones) discusses the joys of plumbing with Adam Belinski (Charles Boyer).

autobiographical bent. *The Tempest,* for one, is generally considered Shakespeare's farewell to the Elizabethan stage (although it was not the last play he had a hand in), and Prospero, the play's exiled intellectual-cum-sorcerer, is generally considered something of a self-portrait: the old artist who comes finally to understand the nature and limits of his art, the nature and limits of humanity, a man who comes to understand that life is an insubstantial pageant rounded by a sleep, a pageant enlivened by love and imagination, a pageant threatened by mortality and corruptability. It is this awareness of mortality, and the responsibility demanded of mortal men, that encourages Prospero to give up his magic, to yield up his book and staff, and to return, as Shakespeare did, to the place of his birth.

In many ways, then, *Cluny Brown* is the Lubitsch *Tempest,* a fanciful glance at the mortal condition in which the artist reflects upon the nature and value of his art. Lubitsch accomplishes the reflection after Shakespeare's fashion, by having the main character serve as a surrogate self. Like Lubitsch, Adam Belinski (Charles Boyer) is a mid-European exile, with a foreign name, a foreign accent (although Boyer sounds more like Chevalier than Lubitsch), and an exile's lack of security. That security is further threatened, as was Prospero's, by the animosity of Belinski's oppressor, in this case Adolf Hitler. Belinski's response to his situation is a relaxed one; his magic, such as it is, is used only to borrow a few pounds and a dinner jacket; and hence he is not, as Prospero was, concerned to punish his enemies. On the contrary, Belinski's real problem in the film has little to do with his enemies. It has more to do with his friends. Belinski is beset by the foibles of the

Wild in the country: Katharine Hepburn, Cary Grant, and George the dog in *Bringing Up Baby* by Howard Hawks.

English gentry, and he must do his humorous best to survive under the circumstances.

Those circumstances seem, at first glance, remarkably similar to those in the Howard Hawks comedy *Bringing Up Baby,* although the issues are somewhat reversed. Like David Huxly (Cary Grant), Belinski goes from the city, where he feels at home, to the country, where he feels somewhat out of place ("place" is a key-word in *Cluny Brown*). The film's major actions, then, and accordingly its major issues, are enacted and resolved in a country setting. But note how the Lubitsch countryside differs from that of Hawks. In Hawks, the countryside is alive with moonlight, crazy adventures, and even crazier people. Indeed, David finds himself involved with a certifiably loony family, the point being that David needs to let the lunacy rub off on him. He needs to leave his dignity aside in order to let his true humanity come to full expression. Thus it is the exiled city boy who must come to his comic senses. The countryside will doubtless stay vital forever.

In Lubitsch, on the other hand, it is not primarily the lead character who needs changing, though Belinski does change and is the better man for it, but the country, which has become somewhat overgrown with custom and tradition. The "greenworld" of *Cluny Brown* is not a wood full of dogs, bones, and leopards; but instead is a sculptured English garden, carefully trimmed and governed by Lady Carmel (Margaret Bannerman). There seems little place for squirrels or nuts; and indeed we are uncertain that there is sufficient place for the vitality and humour of a Cluny Brown (Jennifer Jones) or an Adam Belinski. In an odd way, then, the natural people, the squirrel people and the cat people (remember Cluny's drunken Ninotchka-like soliloquy in the film's first scene), seem out of place in nature.

The extent to which this natural vitality is lacking at and around the Carmel estate is made clear by the chemist, Mr. Wilson (Richard Haydn), and his mumbling mother, who is always clearing her throat. Wilson is characterised by two extreme desires, desires which are, in their extremity, mutually exclusive. On the one hand he wants a wife, a wife vital enough to bear a brood of well-mannered little Wilsons. But, on the other hand, as he tells Cluny on the occasion of her first visit to his "castle," Wilson also wants complete and unassailable security, a rock-hard status quo. He wants to live and die in that one well-ordered house, and he tries to protect himself and his house against all encroachments, against clients, fires, even against enthusiastic young ladies who enjoy a bit of plumbing now and again (Cluny is a plumber's niece, after all). Wilson is thus caught in a bourgeois sort of "Catch 22." No woman vital enough to revitalize the Wilson blood ever stands a chance of getting past the Wilson defenses. Lubitsch lets us see all of

137

The Wilson castle: Richard Haydn, Jennifer Jones, and Una O'Connor in *Cluny Brown*.

this deftly and precisely: the nasal twang of Wilson's speech, the parlour with its map and harmonium, the shop walls lined with bottles, all evidence the sheepishly self-destructive complacency of the British middle-class.

But the clarity of the Lubitsch vision shows us something else as well. Wilson is more to be pitied than scorned. Witness his humiliation at his mother's birthday party when Cluny Brown rolls up her sleeves and checks the bathroom pipes. The pained expression on Wilson's face when he sees Cluny Brown ride by on the handlebars of the delivery boy's bicycle further evidences his profound disappointment, a semi-conscious awareness that life is literally passing him by. Wilson is a solitary English sheep in a barren field, and he senses the futility of his life: at best he is mutton for Her Majesty's economy.

The depths of Lubitsch's understanding are made even clearer when we turn to the Carmel household. Wilson is, after all, an extreme case, and one who arouses, therefore, an unusual sort of pity. The Carmel household, on the other hand, is certainly plagued by many of the same preconceptions that affect Wilson, yet the Carmels also have a resiliency, a vitality, of their own. Thus Lubitsch does not have to worry overmuch about them. He can sit back and observe with confident but concerned amusement.

The primary characteristic of the Carmel household is a humorously graceful sense of propriety. Most of the humour comes from Sir Henry (Reginald Owen) and his apparently dim wits, his thinking that *Mein Kampf* is a boy scout manual: "My Camp", for example. Most of the grace flows from Lady Carmel. She is charming, kind, and pleasant, even to inexperienced servants like Cluny Brown; and if her gestures are not always appropriate (she puts a nightingale under the bird-hating Belinski's window), at least her motives are admirable. She is genuinely concerned for Belinski's physical and spiritual welfare. Most of the propriety, in turn, comes from the housekeeper and the butler, those two rock-solid symbols of British virtue. They are, as Belinski himself tells us, the guardians of English custom and tradition; and as befits such guardians of past glories, the housekeeper and the butler are unlikely to accept change of even the slightest sort.

It is this disinclination to accept change that is the film's real issue. In this context, Hitler and his dreams of Nineteenth-century Prussian supremacy serve as an archetype of social rigidity and repression. Hitler wanted to return Germany to the glories of its feudal past by re-imposing a feudal social structure—something which the British characters themselves never seriously consider. The British may believe in a cozy sort of class structure, but they never long for the days of absolute monarchy. For all of its stolidity, the British way of life is a way of *life,* not a way of death, unless carried to Wilson's extremes. Thus, with the exception of the pitiful and rather harmless chemist, there is no single character *within* the film who presents any sort of clear and present danger to continued existence.

The little danger that there is takes two primary forms. The first is British complacency, a somewhat justifiable sense of self-satisfaction which believes writing letters to the "Times," as young Andrew (Peter Lawford) does, a sufficiently daring moral act. The problem with this attitude is that it lacks a proper sense of vigilance: because it is so self-contained it may fail to be aware of external threats of the Nazi variety. The second problem is just the reverse and involves a lack of self-confidence. Andrew is afraid of proposing to Betty Cream (Helen Walker) because he fears she will reject him. Similarly, Cluny Brown fears any attachment with Belinski. He is clearly her type, the "squirrels to the nuts" type; in her dreams, indeed, Belinski is a desert prince on a "black stallion" who "swoops" her up and carries her away. But Cluny forces Belinski to swear a pact of platonic fealty for fear of going too far too soon and hence losing him forever.

What is needed, then, is something to shake things up a bit, something to rattle people back into their senses. That something is Belinski. He is the one who speaks to servants, who points out that lean mutton really is preferable to fat mutton, who tells Betty Cream that marriage to idealistic young Andrew is far preferable to spinsterhood. Belinski is the man of tact and foresight who can quote Shakespeare to Englishmen (the "other Eden" speech from *Richard II,* and the "quality of mercy" speech from *The Merchant of Venice*) and bring it off gracefully. Belinski is, like Lubitsch himself, a comic artist who takes great joy in humanity; and he does the best he can to give humanity both the necessary kick in the pants and the room to move after the kicking is done. Also like Lubitsch, Belinski is forced, through the exercise of his art, to consider the meaning and the function of the artist.

For most of the film Belinski stands outside the action, coming through a window or door on occasion to give advice or ask a nudging question. Like Shakespeare's Oberon, he plays the role of puppeteer, pulling strings as tactfully as possible, so tactfully that people seldom notice. In his own way, then, Belinski is just as settled into his character of moral philosopher as Mr. Wilson is settled into his character of a chemist. So the question arises, both in our mind and Belinski's, whether disinterested action, however correct, is sufficiently humane. Can Belinski just sit back and tell others to loosen up and get involved, or must he get involved himself?

The answer is clear. He must and, to his great credit, does. After the inhabitants of the Carmel household are brought to their relative senses, Belinski decides in his mysterious way to leave. By now even the servants are on speaking terms with their guest, Andrew and Betty Cream are finally engaged, both Andrew and Sir Henry are aware of the likelihood of war, and even Lady Carmel seems to have a greater sense of urgency. There is only one thing left to do, and that is to rescue Cluny Brown. No matter how rejuvenated the Carmel household might be, it is still no place for a squirrel person like Cluny Brown. It is unclear, and probably unimportant, whether Belinski in any way consciously planned her escape. But once Cluny catches him on the depot platform, Belinski is faced with a clear choice, to continue his vagabond bachelorhood, writing philosophical tracts that only his enemies will read; or marry Cluny Brown, write popular novels that

The Carmel household: Sir Henry (Reginald Owen), Betty Cream (Helen Walker), Andrew (Peter Lawford), Cluny Brown (Jennifer Jones), and Lady Alice (Margaret Bannerman).

everyone will read *(The Nightingale Strikes Again),* and father a brood of plumbing little Belinskis. The choice is an easy one: Belinski chooses involvement rather than detachment, chooses a truly sexual, hence social, hence comic existence rather than a life of solitary exile. Therefore the end of the film, with Belinski and a pregnant Cluny Brown back among the people, within society, on the streets of New York City, is the perfect conclusion to the Lubitsch career. As Belinski tells Cluny at the beginning of the film, "wherever you are happy, that's your place." And Lubitsch valued human happiness above all else.

Conclusion

Criticism, as I profess and practice it, operates between extremes of description and generalisation. As an act of comprehension, criticism seeks to construct a bridge between the two, thus to link experience (the film we see) with history (the films we remember and feel compelled to talk about). It is impossible to reconstruct a film; no such reconstruction, even a frame by frame description, can substitute for the film itself. Such descriptions are only helpful as aids to understanding: they are, quite literally, notes. Criticism must go beyond the stage of notation to deal with the more difficult task of integration—at which point the critic scans his notes and recollections and begins to offer, as I have repeatedly offered here, "readings," after-the-fact statements which gain in truth what they lose in detail. In other words, a critic will build a case, citing quite selectively from a wealth of detail, for the purpose of "making sense" of otherwise chaotic and ephemeral recollections.

Paradoxically, however, critical generalisations of the sort offered here tend very often to aid recollection. To begin with, while critics do not and cannot cite all possible evidence, they necessarily cite some, and (excepting inaccuracies) even modest detail tends to bring to mind additional information. More importantly, however, the conceptual framework generated by criticism gives form and purpose to our recollections, attaching genuine significance to otherwise insignificant, perhaps forgotten or misunderstood, details. Thus, while criticism begins as a process of abstraction, it generally leads to an enriched sense of film history, which leads in turn to an enriched capacity for film appreciation. In other words, and it bears repeating, knowledge begets knowledge.

The community of scholars in *Sumurun*.

Debates about the function and purpose of film criticism can generally be located somewhere in the area between detail and generalisation. *Auteur* criticism, for example, argues the case for purposeful generality. This can clearly be seen, in retrospect, as a reaction against the amorphousness of "impressionistic" film criticism of the Otis Ferguson sort. To be sure, Ferguson and others like him (MacDonald, Kauffmann, Kael) fulfill a useful function—as reviewers. But film reviewing is generally a hit or miss proposition, governed by chance (the run of current releases) and the demands of popular journalism (the necessity for brief, flashy copy).

Auteurism, on the other hand, proposes a definite principle by which to select texts for analysis. Rather than scan the current scene, the *auteur* critic takes the proper subject of study to be the career of a

143

specific film-maker. Usually, "film-maker" is understood to be the director (as for Sarris) but increasingly we have come to talk of other kinds of *auteurs*—screenwriters (as Corliss urges), producers, actors and others. In every case, however, the subject of analysis is a career rather than a single film. Therefore, the *auteur* theory encourages a high degree of generalisation. A journal article on, say, the films of John Ford can hardly avoid operating at a level of abstraction often far removed from the details of camera placement, editing or lighting. It is important to argue, however, that the validity of such an article does not depend upon any one kind of evidence: it is just as useful to discuss Ford's plots and characters as it is to consider his propensity for horizon shots and tableau-like group portraits. The only legitimate objection to the citation of a particular sort of evidence is that it does not exist (if Ford has characters in his films, they are fair game for discussion). Likewise, the only legitimate objection to a certain critical generalisation is that it falsifies the evidence. This is true even in those cases where knowledge of supporting evidence is merely assumed (as Sarris assumes some degree of knowledge in the reader of *The American Cinema*). The problem here, of course, is that critics addicted to the grand generality tend simply to ignore evidence altogether.

My objection to Weinberg's treatment of Lubitsch, therefore, is based primarily on practical considerations. The reality of academic politics is such that Weinberg-like generalisations—however accurate they may be (and my own study does not seriously contradict Weinberg)—are unlikely to be tested. I believe, however, that Lubitsch deserves to be widely and seriously studied, and Weinberg's panegyrics are likely to discourage scholars by seeming too facile. The advantage of citing detailed evidence of every sort (characters, themes, structural patterns, visual figures) is that copious evidence lends weight and believability, especially when marshalled in the service of a controversial thesis. And often, and particularly with Lubitsch, there is a tendency to mistake a fluid style for a facile imagination.

Semiological film criticism, in its turn, can be understood as a reaction against the abstractness of auteurism. The semiological concern with codes of enunciation directs attention to very specific cinematic patterns—of physical gesture, of camera movement, of editing, of lighting, and so on. The problems with semiology are many, and are too complex to pursue here. The impulses behind the rise of semiology, however, are fairly readily understood. By avoiding abstraction semiologists sought to avoid the trap of culture. If it were possible to objectify the "science" of criticism, by operating at the level of notation, then the critic's "ideological" bias could be avoided. The difficulty, of course, is that notation remains notation—a denatured

Trouble in Paradise: **Herbert Marshall, Kay Francis and Charlie Ruggles.**

transcript of the film itself. Notation cannot integrate or comprehend.

Semiology has had a positive effect, however, by challenging the assumption that casual criticism is possible. The semiological passion for accurate description effectively discourages the sort of carelessness about evidence that has often characterised film scholarship. However, a genuine act of criticism must go beyond accurate description to significant insight, must go beyond detail to generalisation. Here too we have a practical problem. A copiously detailed analysis of a specific film—however admirable an enterprise—requires extended access to prints and a sympathetic publisher willing to devote copious space to a single article on a single film (see Stephen Heath's lengthy *critique* of *Touch of Evil* in "Screen," for example). Indeed, a shot-by-shot analysis of a film-maker's entire output is a practical impossibility from a publishing point-of-view. Hence my continued allegiance to an extended form of auteurism. I believe that an essay such as this one, which steers a middle course between the general and the specific, remains the most profitable form of critical enterprise.

I have therefore endeavoured to achieve a workable compromise between criticism and meta-criticism. Criticism, in this sense of the word, which I employ to refer to a specific level of abstraction, is concerned to "read" specific films. This process of reading is quite familiar and derives its methodology and terminology from literary New Criticism. It considers themes, characters, images, symbols, sounds, settings, as they work together to express a vision of value and experience. The rhetoric here is the rhetoric of fiction, which I take to be fairly (though not completely) constant across media. The goal is to

Gary Cooper and Claudette Colbert in *Bluebeard's Eighth Wife.*

146

Dietrich and Lubitsch.

arrive at readings which are intuitively in accord with the "grammar" of each film. Ideally, a person who has seen one or more of the films under discussion will remark upon reading this essay—"yes, that really is how *The Merry Widow* works." This sort of criticism requires attention to specific cinematic detail—how scenes are enacted and staged and to what purpose—but that attention need not necessarily be expressed by lengthy discussion of, say, editing in *To Be or Not To Be*. Indeed, one point of this essay has been to demonstrate the increasing futility of discussing Lubitsch solely in the context of "pure cinema." The more one studies Lubitsch the clearer it becomes that form really does follow function, and the function of Lubitsch's later films became increasingly the expression of an other-centred, if not self-effacing, humanism.

Which is not to say that Lubitsch lost his "touch." It argues, rather, that his "touch" can best be understood in the context of his larger concerns. Indeed, the study of narrative and theme serves finally to clarify our understanding of style. I have argued generally that Lubitsch seeks not to overturn social conventions but to renew them. Thus in *Heaven Can Wait* we see that the conventional, as personified by Albert, and the unconventional, as personified by Henry, are necessary complements: each lends value to the other. A similar relationship exists between the conventional and unconventional elements in the Lubitsch style. Like Henry Van Cleve, Lubitsch always feels free to indulge a certain stylistic whimsicality—not for the sake of mere self-indulgence—but because he knows that even a little whimsicality lends a certain flavour to otherwise conventional modes of behaviour. When watching a Lubitsch film, we tend to anticipate the unusual shot, the unusual camera movement, the unusual editing figure. Yet that very anticipation effectively acknowledges the purpose behind even the most simple two-shot. If Lubitsch could have shot it otherwise, which we never doubt, then his decision to shoot it straight must be taken as genuinely expressive, as is repeatedly and increasingly the case in his later films. Thus Lubitsch was never the slave of convention, no matter how conventional his style eventually became. He was always the master.

At this point we are engaging in the practice of meta-criticism. If criticism *per se* reads shots and scenes in order to arrive at an understanding of specific films, then meta-criticism reads specific films in order to arrive at an understanding of a particular cinematic career. Thus I have attempted to discern and describe constant structural and thematic patterns at work in the American films of Ernst Lubitsch. Again, there is a necessity for selectively citing evidence. I have not referred to every film that Lubitsch made in America: that would be

The Master—then, now, and always.

impossible. Yet I believe that the present work, however tentative its conclusions, will make it easier for students, scholars, and audiences to understand and value the cinema of Ernst Lubitsch. Such is the function of film criticism, and I am convinced that Lubitsch more than justifies our efforts.

Notes and Bibliography

[1] Theodore Huff, *An Index to the Films of Ernst Lubitsch* (London: The British Film Institute, 1947), p. 13.

[2] Gerald Mast, *The Comic Mind: Comedy and the Movies* (New York: Bobbs-Merrill, 1973), p. 211

[3] Richard Corliss, *Talking Pictures* (Woodstock, N.Y.: Overlook Press, 1974), p. 172.

[4] Charles Silver makes the point in *Marlene Dietrich* (New York: Pyramid, 1974), p. 87. Silver's section on *Angel* is excellent. I have not seen the film, but on the basis of Silver's description it sounds very similar to *Lady Windermere's Fan*—with Dietrich's "Angel" playing the Mrs. Erlynne role.

[5] John Baxter makes a similar point in "Some Lubitsch Silents," *The Silent Picture*, No. 11/12 (1971).

[6] Patrick Brion, "Old Heidelberg," *Cahiers du Cinéma*, No. 198 (1968), p. 37, (my translation).

[7] See Jean-Loup Bourget, "Muted Strings: Ernst Lubitsch's *Broken Lullaby*," *Monogram*, No. 5 (1974), pp. 24-26.

[8] Nancy Schwartz, "Lubitsch's Widow: The Meaning of a Waltz," *Film Comment*," 11, No. 2 (1975), p. 14.

[9] F. Dufour, "Lubitsch: l'être et le paraître," *Cinéma* (Paris), No. 177 (1973), pp. 74-78.

[10] For a while it remained questionable whether Lubitsch or Cukor actually directed *One Hour with You* [see, for example, Andrew Sarris, "Lubitsch in the Thirties—Part One," *Film Comment*, 7, No. 4 (1971), p. 55]. Cukor settled the question in the *On Cukor* (New York: Capricorn, 1973) interview when he told Gavin Lambert that "Lubitsch really directed it" (p. 43). Cukor had started the film, but after two weeks of shooting Lubitsch more or less took over, only occasionally asking Cukor to lend a well-supervised hand.

[11] Richard Koszarski, "On *Trouble in Paradise*," *Film Comment* 6, No. 3 (1970), p. 47.

[12] Mast, op. cit. p. 219.

[13] Graham Petrie, "Theatre Film Life," *Film Comment*, 10, No. 3 (1974), p. 38.

^{14}See Sigmund Freud, *Jokes and Their Relation to the Unconscious*, trans. James Strachey (New York: W. W. Norton, 1963) and Arthur Koestler, *The Act of Creation: A Study of the Conscious and Unconscious in Science and Art* (New York: Dell, 1967).

^{15}Corliss makes much the same point in *Talking Pictures*, p. 305.

^{16}The Museum of Modern Art print of *So This Is Paris* has French titles—my translations.

^{17}Mast. op. cit. p. 215.

^{18}John Baxter, *Hollywood in the Thirties* (New York: A. S. Barnes London: Tantivy Press, 1968), p. 57.

^{19}It is worth a footnote to point out that Henry's description of love as an "electric spark" recalls similar remarks by Gilda in *Design for Living* and Leon in *Ninotchka*.

A Bibliographical Note

Most of the recent scholarship on Lubitsch is summarised above. It should be mentioned, however, that "Cahiers du Cinéma," 198 (1968), is largely devoted to Lubitsch and is not limited to Brion's discussion of *The Student Prince*. See as well "Positif," 137 (1972), for Frédéric Vitoux's "Ernst Lubitsch, Le maître." I should also point out that the second part of Sarris's "Lubitsch in the Thirties" appeared in "Film Comment," 8, No. 2 (1972). Raymond Durgnat treats Lubitsch at some length in *The Crazy Mirror* (New York: Horizon, 1969), as do Molly Haskell in *From Reverence to Rape* (New York: Holt, Rinehart and Winston, 1974), Andrew Bergman in *We're in the Money: Depression America and Its Films* (1971; reprint. New York: Harper and Row, 1972) and Peter Bogdanovich in *Pieces of Time* (New York: Arbor House, 1973). An excellent article by Neil D. Isaacs on "Lubitsch and the Filmed-Play Syndrome" appeared after the completion of this manuscript in "Literature/Film Quarterly," 3, No. 4 (1975), and Robin Wood discusses *To Be or Not To Be* in "Acting Up" in "Film Comment," 12, No. 2 (1976). Jan-Christopher Horak has written a master's thesis for Boston University on Lubitsch's German films, part of which has been published as "The Pre-Hollywood Lubitsch" in "Image," 18, No. 4 (1975). Readers might also wish to consult William K. Everson's review of Herman G. Weinberg's *The Lubitsch Touch* (New York: E. P. Dutton & Co., 1968) in "Film Library Quarterly," 2, No. 2 (1969). Further bibliographical references are to be found by consulting the lengthy bibliography in *The Lubitsch Touch*. Weinberg is fairly exhaustive up to 1968, particularly in his listing of reviews.

Ernst Lubitsch Filmography

Note: This filmography is primarily a collation of information from three previously published works: 1) "An Index to the Films of Ernst Lubitsch" by Theodore Huff (London: "Sight and Sound"/British Film Institute Index Series No. 9, January 1947); 2) "Biofilmographie d'Ernst Lubitsch" by Patrick Brion (Paris: "Cahiers du Cinéma," No. 198, February 1968); and 3) *The Lubitsch Touch: A Critical Study* by Herman Weinberg (New York: E. P. Dutton, 1968). As such it is basically conservative; it seeks to rectify and clarify certain errors of omission and commission of the previous works, and to present in/as accurate a form as possible material from widely separate and difficult-to-come-by sources. The Huff pamphlet has been long out of print and is a rare item. Over and above this, the format is a proofreader's nightmare and, though the work is basically sound as to dates and titles, other information such as names is suspect as to spelling, etc.; furthermore, Huff's work was done nearly a year before Lubitsch's death and so there is no information whatever on *That Lady in Ermine.* Weinberg presents a dual problem for the scholar. First, his book is not "critical" as his subtitle implies, but primarily anecdotal; he knew Lubitsch well and his text is a labour of love more than scholarship. Second, Weinberg's filmography is "radical": several films of the 1913-1918 period he merely lists without citing evidence or definite sources of information, and in credits he tends to put in names and information which the other compilers either do not mention or qualify with a question mark. Of the three, the Brion filmography is probably the most reliable. Brion is closer to primary resources, especially concerning Lubitsch's early career as actor and director, and he gives complete information on those films with which Lubitsch was associated either as one director among many *(If I Had a Million),* or as producer *(Desire, Dragonwyck).* Our filmography gives only information on which a majority of our sources agree.

* * *

Ernst Lubitsch was born on January 28th, 1892 in Berlin. In his teens he was introduced to the popular German stage comedian Victor Arnold, who became his acting teacher. In 1911, Arnold introduced Lubitsch to Max Reinhardt who hired

him as an actor. Among Lubitsch's stage credits are "Faust," "Das Mirakel," and "Sumurun." During his theatrical apprenticeship Lubitsch supplemented his meagre earnings by working a variety of jobs in the fledgling German film industry.
In 1913 Lubitsch quit the stage to enter the movies as an actor and comic. [The date is of more than biographical interest. In her definitive study of the German silent cinema, *L'Ecran Demoniaque* (published in America as *The Haunted Screen* [Berkeley: University of California Press, 1969]), Lotte H. Eisner sets this date as the true beginning of the German film as an art-form.]

I. *Lubitsch in Germany*
   A. *As an actor*
DAS MIRAKEL (1912). A filmed version of Max Reinhardt's London stage production of "The Miracle," directed by Reinhardt and featuring Lubitsch in the cast.

VENEZIANISCHE NÄCHTE (Venetian Nights, 1912). Written and directed by Reinhardt expressly for the screen, again with Lubitsch in the cast.

MEYER AUF DER ALM (Meyer in the Alps, 1913). Lubitsch's debut as a film comic.

DIE FIRMA HEIRATAT (The Firm Marries, 1914).

DER STOLZ DER FIRMA (The Pride of the Firm, 1914).

FRAÜLEIN SEIFENSCHAUM (Miss Soapsuds, 1914).

MEYER ALS SOLDAT (Meyer As a Soldier, 1914).

ARME MARIE! (Poor Marie, 1915).

   B. *As director or as actor and director*
BLINDE KUH (Blind Cow, 1915). The first film conclusively known to be directed by Lutitsch, although he may have directed *Fräulein Seifenschaum* (Weinberg, p. 298).

(Unless otherwise noted, all subsequent films are directed by Lubitsch.)

AUF EIS GEFÜHRT (A Trip On the Ice, 1915).

ZUCKER UND ZIMT (Sugar and Cinnamon, 1915).

WO IST MEIN SCHATZ? (Where is My Treasure, 1916).

DER SCHWARZE MORITZ (Black Moritz, 1916). A combination of stage and film musical-comedy, with Lubitsch appearing in blackface.

SCHUHPALAST PINKUS (Shoepalace Pinkus, 1916). *Sc:* Hans Kräly, Erich Schönfelder. Lubitsch's first "hit," and first notable collaboration with writer Hans Kräly. Lubitsch played the title role.

DER GEMISCHTE FRAUENCHOR (The Mixed Ladies' Chorus, 1916).

DER G.M.B.H. TENOR (Tenor, Incorporated, 1916).

OSSIS TAGEBUCH (Ossi's Diary, 1917). *With* Ossi Oswalda.

DER BLUSENKÖNIG (The Blouse King, 1917).

WENN VIER DASSELBE TUN (When Four Do the Same, 1917). *With* Ossi Oswalda, Emil Jannings.

DAS FIDELE GEFÄNGNIS (The Merry Prison, 1917). Based upon the Johann Strauss operetta "Die Fledermaus." *With* Ossi Oswalda, Emil Jannings, Lubitsch.

PRINZ SAMI (Prince Sami, 1918).

DER RODELKAVALIER (The Toboggan Cavalier, 1918).

DER FALL ROSENTOPF (The Rosentopf Case, 1918).

ICH MÖCHTE KEIN MANN SEIN (I Don't Want To Be a Man, 1918 or 1919). Listed by Weinberg (p. 302) who also says that a print exists at George Eastman House, Rochester, New York.

DIE AUGEN DER MUMIE MA (The Eyes of the Mummy Ma, 1918). An Egyptian religious fanatic pursues and eventually destroys the beautiful temple dancer who deserted him for an English painter. *Sc:* Hans Kräly. *Ph:* Alfred Hanson. *Sets:* Kurt Richter. *With* Pola Negri *(Mara, the dancer)*, Emil Jannings *(Radu, the fanatic)*, Harry Liedtke *(Wendland, the painter)*, Max Laurence *(Duke of Hohenfels)*. *Prod:* Union. (Released in America as *The Eyes of the Mummy* by Paramount, 1922). 55m. Lubitsch's first feature-length film.

DAS MÄDEL VOM BALLET (The Ballet Girl, 1918).

CARMEN (1918). A hot-blooded gypsy girl destroys herself and the genteel young man who falls for her. *Sc:* Hans Kräly, from the story by Prosper Mérimée. *Ph:* Theodor Sparkuhl. *Sets:* Karl Machus. *With* Pola Negri *(Carmen)*, Harry Liedtke *(Don Jose)*, Magnus Sifter *(Escamillo)*. *Prod:* Union-Ufa. (Released in America as *Gypsy Blood* by First National, 1921.) 60m.

MEYER AUS BERLIN (Meyer from Berlin, 1918).

MEINE FRAU, DIE FILMSCHAUSPIELERIN (My Wife, the Movie Star, 1919).

SCHWABENMÄDIE (The Swabian Girl, 1919).

DIE AUSTERNPRINZESSIN (The Oyster Princess, 1919). A satirical view of rich Americans abroad who clash with old world aristocracy in their attempts to purchase a title. *Sc:* Hans Kräly, Lubitsch. *Ph:* Theodore Sparkuhl. *Sets:* Ernst Stern, Emil Hasler, Karl Machus. *With* Ossi Oswalda *(the "Princess")*, Victor Janson *(Quaker, the American "Oyster King," her father)*, Harry Liedtke *(Prince Nuki)*, Julius Falkenstein, Kurt Bois. *Prod:* Union. (Not released in America.) 70 m.

RAUSCH (Intoxication, 1919). A young artist in love with a beautiful sculptress wishes that his illegitimate child by a previous mistress did not exist. When the child dies, he is charged with her murder. However, after it is determined that the death was a natural one, the artist still considers himself guilty—for the thought, if not the

Pola Negri (left) in *Carmen*.

deed. (This summary is extracted from the play on which the film was based; details about the film itself are incomplete.) *Sc:* Hans Kräly, from the play "There Are Crimes and Crimes" by August Strindberg. *With* Asta Nielsen, Alfred Abel, Karl Meinhard. *Prod:* Argus-Film. 5 reels.

MADAME DUBARRY (1919). An historical spectacle recounting the notorious lady's sexual conquest of Louis XV amid the social turmoil and political intrigue that climaxes in the French Revolution. The film ends with DuBarry's death on the guillotine. *Sc:* Fred Orbing, Hans Kräly. *Ph:* Theodor Sparkuhl. *Cost:* Ali Hubert. *Tech. Advisor:* Kurt Waschneck. *With* Pola Negri *(Madame DuBarry)*, Emil Jannings *(Louis XV)*, Harry Liedtke *(Armand de Foix)*, Eduard von Winterstein *(Jean DuBarry)*, Reinhold Schunzel *(Duc de Choiseul)*, Elsa Berna *(Duchesse de Grammont)*, Frederich Immler *(Duc de Richelieu)*, Gustav Czimeg *(Duc d'Aiguillon)*, Carl Platen *(Guillaume DuBarry)*. *Prod:* Union-Ufa. (Released in America as *Passion* by First National, 1920.) 85m. (The first of a series of historical spectacles concentrating on the love lives of famous personages that would earn Lubitsch fame as the "Humanizer of History." More significantly, *Madame DuBarry* was the first post-war German film to be distributed in the United States.)

Pola Negri (center) as *Madame DuBarry*.

DIE PUPPE (The Doll, 1919). In order to win an inheritance, a misogynistic young man purchases a "wife" in the form of a lifesize doll. When the doll is broken, the dollmaker's daughter takes its place. The two young people fall in love and marry, and the young man gets his money. *Sc:* Hans Kräly. *Ph:* Theodor Sparkuhl. *Sets:* Kurt Richter. *Tech. Advisor:* Kurt Waschneck. *With* Ossi Oswalda *(The Doll),* Victor Janson *(Hilarius, the dollmaker),* Hermann Thimig *(Lancelot von Chanterelle),* Max Kronert *(Baron von Chanterelle),* Marga Köhler *(Hilarius's wife),* Gerhard Ritterband *(apprentice),* Jakob Tiedtke *(Prior). Prod:* Union-Ufa. (Due to censorship problems over its supposedly anti-clerical content, *Die Puppe* was not released in America until 1928.) 60 m.

KOHLHIESELS TOCHTER (Kohlhiesel's Daughters, 1920). A peasant comedy involving two daughters, one beautiful, the other not, and a "dumb ox" farm hand. *Sc:* Hans Kräly, Lubitsch. *Ph:* Theodore Sparkuhl. *Sets:* Hans Winter. *With* Henny Porten *(Gretl and Liesl, the daughters),* Emil Jannings *(Peer Xavero),* Jakob Tiedtke *(Mathias Kohlhiesel),* Gustav von Wagenheim *(Paul). Prod:* Messter-Union-Ufa. (Not released in America.) 70m.

ROMEO UND JULIA IM SCHNEE (Romeo and Juliet In the Snow, 1920). Lubitsch's last short comedy.

157

Pola Negri and Paul Wegener (left and center) in *Sumurun.*

SUMURUN (1920). An "Arabian Nights" melodrama in which an old sheik and his son vie for the love of Sumurun, the sheik's favourite wife. The plot is further complicated by a dancer's love for the son, and a hunchback's love for the dancer. *Sc:* Hans Kräly, Lubitsch, from the stage pantomime by Friedrich Freska and Victor Holländer. *Ph:* Theodor Sparkuhl. *Sets:* Kurt Richter, Erno Metzner. *Cost:* Ali Hubert. *Tech. Advisor:* Kurt Waschneck. *With* Pola Negri *(Yannaia, the dancer),* Ernst Lubitsch *(Yeggar, the hunchback),* Paul Wegener *(The Sheik),* Jenny Hasselquist *(Zuleika, or "Sumurun"),* Aud Egede Nissen *(Haidee),* Harry Liedtke *(Nur-Al-Din, a Merchant),* Carl Clewing *(The Sheik's Son),* Paul Biensfeldt *(Slave Dancer),* Margarete Kupfer *(Old Woman),* Jakob Tiedtke *(Chief Eunuch). Prod:* Union-Ufa. (Released in America as *One Arabian Night* by First National, 1921.) 90m.

ANNA BOLEYN (Anne Boleyn, 1920). Another historical romance, set in England, recounting Anne's rise; her sexual intrigues as Henry VIII's second wife; and her downfall and death when Henry courts Jane Seymour. *Sc:* Fred Orbing, Hans

Kräly. *Ph:* Theodor Sparkuhl. *Sets:* Kurt Richter. *Cost:* Ali Hubert. *With:* Henny Porten *(Anne Boleyn),* Emil Jannings *(Henry VIII),* Aud Egede Nissen *(Jane Seymour),* Paul Hartmann *(Henry Norris),* Ludwig Hartau, Ferdinand von Alten, Paul Biensfeldt, Wilhelm Diegelmann, Friedrich Kühne, Maria Reisenhofer, Hedwig Pauli. *Prod:* Union-Ufa. (Released in America as *Deception* by Paramount, 1921.)

DIE BERGKATZE (The Mountain Cat *or* The Wildcat, 1921). A blend of anti-militarist satire and comic romance, involving a brigand, his daughter, and the local garrison. *Sc:* Hans Kräly, Lubitsch. *Ph:* Theodor Sparkuhl. *Sets:* Ernst Stern. *With* Pola Negri *(Rischka, the "Wildcat"),* Victor Janson *(Commander of Fort Tossenstein),* Paul Heidemann *(Lt. Alexis),* Wilhelm Diegelmann *(Claudius, Rischka's father),* Hermann Thimig *(Pepo),* Edith Meller *(Lilli),* Margarete Köhler *(Commander's wife),* Paul Graetz *(Zorfano),* Paul Biensfeldt *(Dafko),* Max Kronert *(Masilio),* Erwin Kropp *(Tripo).* *Prod:* Union-Ufa. (Not released in America.) 100m.

Emil Jannings and Henny Porten in *Anna Boleyn.*

159

The Wife of Pharaoh (1921).

DAS WEIB DES PHARAO (The Wife of Pharaoh, 1921). Egypt and Ethiopia war over a slave girl, only to have her reject both monarchs in favor of Ramphis, her true love. *Sc:* Norbert Falk, Hans Kräly. *Ph:* Theodor Sparkuhl, Alfred Hansen. *Sets:* Erno Metzner, Ernst Stern, Kurt Richter. *Cost:* Ali Hubert. *Tech. Advisor:* Max Gronau. *Mus:* Eduard Künneke. *With* Emil Jannings *(Pharaoh),* Harry Liedtke *(Ramphis),* Dagny Servaes *(Theonis, the slave girl),* Paul Wegener *(Samlak, King of Ethiopia),* Lyda Salmonova *(Makeda, Samlak's daughter),* Albert Bassermann *(Sotis),* Friedrich Kühne *(High Priest),* Paul Biensfeldt *(Menon). Prod:* Efa-Ufa. (Released in America as *The Loves of Pharaoh* by Paramount, 1922.) 6 reels.

DIE FLAMME (The Flame, 1922). A tragic fable about a doomed love affair between a Parisian prostitute and a composer. After they are married, she desparately attempts to adjust to a new bourgeois life, but commits suicide when she finds herself unable to do so. *Sc:* Hans Kräly, from the play "Die Flamme" by Hans Müller. *Ph:* Theodor Sparkuhl. *With* Pola Negri *(Yvette),* Alfred Abel *(The*

·*Husband)*, Hermann Thimig *(Leduc)*, Hilda Wörner *(Louise)*, Max Adelbert, Frida Richard. *Prod:* Efa-Ufa. (Released in America—with an alternative, "happy" ending—as *Montmartre* by Paramount, 1924.) (Lubitsch's last German film. In December, 1922 he arrived in America under contract to direct a film for Mary Pickford.)

II. *Lubitsch in America*
A. *Silent Films*

ROSITA (1923). In one of her few silent adult roles, Mary Pickford portrays a Spanish streetsinger who attracts the King's attention by lampooning him and subsequently becomes his mistress. Unlike the women in Lubitsch's German films, however, she avoids tragedy and eventually returns to her true love. *Sc:* Edward Knoblock, Hans Kräly, from the play "Don Caesar de Bazan" by Adolphe d'Ennery and P.S.P. Dumanoir. *Ph:* Charles Rosher. *Sets:* Sven Gade. *With* Mary Pickford *(Rosita)*, Holbrook Blinn *(The King)*, Irene Rich *(The Queen)*, George Walsh *(Don Diego)*, Charles Belcher *(Prime Minister)*, Frank Leigh *(Prison Commandant)*, Mathilde Comont *(Rosita's Mother)*, George Periolat *(Rosita's Father)*, Bert Sprotte *(Big Jailer)*, Snitz Edwards *(Little Jailer)*, Mme. de Bodamere *(Servant)*, Phillipe

The Flame (1922).

Mary Pickford as *Rosita* (1923).

DeLacy, Donald McAlpin *(Rosita's Brothers)*, Doreen Turner *(Rosita's Sister)*, Charles Farrell. *Prod:* United Artists-Mary Pickford Co. 85m.

THE MARRIAGE CIRCLE (1924). Two couples, one happily married, the other not, become involved in a comic "circle" of adultery and suspicion which nearly breaks up the happy couple. *Sc:* Paul Bern, from the play "Only a Dream" by Lothar Schmidt. *Ph:* Charles Van Enger. *Sets:* Sven Gade. *With* Florence Vidor (Charlotte Braun), Monte Blue (Dr. Franz Braun), Marie Prevost *(Mizzi Stock)*, Adolphe Menjou *(Prof. Josef Stock)*, Creighton Hale *(Dr. Gustave Müller)*, Harry Myers *(The Detective)*, Dale Fuller. *Prod:* Warner Bros. 8 reels.

The rake and the widow in *Three Women.*

THREE WOMEN (1924). A rake romances a rich, aging widow and her teenaged daughter, while keeping a mistress on the side. *Sc:* Hans Kräly, from an original story by Kräly and Lubitsch. *Ph:* Charles Van Enger. *With* Pauline Frederick *(Mrs. Mabel Wilton)*, May McAvoy *(Jeanne Wilton)*, Marie Prevost *(Harriet)*, Lew Cody *(Edmund Lamont)*, Willard Lewis *(John Howard)*, Pierre Gendron *(Fred Armstrong)*, Mary Carr *(Fred's Mother)*, Raymond McKee *(Harvey Craig)*. *Prod:* Warner Bros. 75m.

FORBIDDEN PARADISE (1924). Catherine the Great of Russia schemes to seduce the handsome young captain who is the *fiancé* of her lady-in-waiting. When she

163

Rod LaRoque and Pola Negri in *Forbidden Paradise* (1924).

fails, Catherine settles for the French Ambassador. *Sc:* Hans Kräly, Agnes Christine Johnstone, from the play "The Czarina" by Lajos Biro and Melchior Lengyel. *Ph:* Charles Van Enger. *Sets:* Hans Dreier. *With* Pola Negri *(Catherine)*, Rod La Roque *(Capt. Alexis Czerny)*, Adolphe Menjou *(Lord Chamberlain)*, Pauline Starke *(Anna, Catherine's Lady-in-waiting)*, Fred Malatesta *(French Ambassador)*, Nick de Ruiz *(The General)*, Carrie D'Aumery *(Lady-in-waiting)*. *Prod:* Paramount. 60m.

KISS ME AGAIN (1925). A dissatisfied wife takes a pianist for a lover. Only after she and her lawyer commence divorce proceedings does she realise that she and her husband really love each other, and they are reconciled. *Sc:* Hans Kräly, from the play "Nous divorçons" by Victorien Sardou and Émile de Najac. *Ph:* Charles Van Enger. *With:* Marie Prevost *(Loulou Fleury)*, Monte Blue *(Gaston Fleury)*, John Roche *(Maurice Ferriere)*, Clara Bow *(Grizette)*, Willard Louis *(DuBois, the lawyer)*. *Prod:* Warner Bros. 7 reels.

LADY WINDERMERE'S FAN (1925). A worldly-wise woman uses her wit and

Emil Jannings in *The Patriot* (1928).

intelligence to save her daughter from scandal when the girl contemplates leaving her husband. *Sc:* Julien Josephson, from the play by Oscar Wilde. *Ph:* Charles Van Enger. *With:* Irene Rich *(Mrs. Erlynne),* May McAvoy *(Lady Windermere),* Ronald Colman *(Lord Darlington),* Bert Lytell *(Lord Windermere),* Edward Martindel *(Lord Augustus),* Helen Dunbar, Carrie D'Aumery, Billie Bennett *(Gossipy Duchesses). Prod:* Warner Bros. 80m.

SO THIS IS PARIS (1926). A husband accidently meets a former love and the old flame begins to rekindle. The amorous mix-ups climax at an impressionistic masked ball, when the drunken husband "picks up" his own wife. *Sc:* Hans Kräly, from the play "Réveillon" by Henri Meilhac and Ludovic Halévy. *Ph:* John Mescall. *With:* Monte Blue *(Dr. Giraud),* Patsy Ruth Miller *(Suzanne Giraud),* Lilyan Tashman *(Georgette Lalle),* André Beranger *(Maurice Lalle),* Myrna Loy *(The Maid),* Sidney D'Albrook *(Cop). Prod:* Warner Bros. 60m.

THE STUDENT PRINCE (1927). The heir to a throne, sent to the University at Heidelberg, delights in the pastoral life and falls in love. However, when the time comes to accept his crown, the Prince sacrifices his ideal life and his sweetheart. *Sc:* Hans Kräly, from the play "Old Heidelberg" by W. Meyerförster, and the operetta

Eternal Love: **Camilla Horn and John Barrymore.**

166

by Dorothy Donelly and Sigmund Romberg. *Ph:* John Mescall. *Sets:* Cedric Gibbons, Richard Day. *Cost:* Ali Hubert. *Ed:* Andrew Marton. *Titles:* Marian Ainslee, Ruth Cummings. *With* Ramon Novarro *(Prince Karl Heinrich)*, Norma Shearer *(Kathi)*, Jean Hersholt *(Dr. Juttner)*, Gustave von Seyffertitz *(King Karl VII)*, Phillippe De Lacy *(Prince Karl, as a child)*, Edgar Norton *(Lutz)*, Bobby Mack *(Kellermann)*, Edward Connelly *(Court Marshall)*, Otis Harlan *(Old Ruder)*, John S. Peters *(Student)*, Edythe Chapman, Lionel Belmore, Lincoln Stedman. *Prod:* Irving Thalberg for Metro-Goldwyn-Mayer. 10 reels. (Some of the love scenes were re-shot by John M. Stahl, and Lubitsch's final edited version was re-edited by Irving Thalberg [Weinberg, p. 319]).

THE PATRIOT (1928). The trusted *confidante* of the insane Czar Paul I becomes a "patriot" by engineering the ruler's assassination for the good of Russia. *Sc:* Hans Kräly, from materials by Alfred Neumann, Ashley Dukes, Dimitri Merejkowski. *Ph:* Bert Glennon. *Sets:* Hans Dreier. *Cost:* Ali Hubert. *Titles:* Julian Johnson. *Mus (Synchronised Score):* Domenico Savino, Gerard Carbonaro. *With* Emil Jannings *(Tsar Paul I)*, Lewis Stone *(Count Pahlen)*, Florence Vidor *(Countess Anna Ostermann)*, Neil Hamilton *(Crown Prince Alexander)*, Harry Cording *(Stefan)*, Vera Veronina *(Mlle. Lapoukhine)*. *Prod:* Ernst Lubitsch for Paramount. 12 reels.

ETERNAL LOVE (1929). During the Napoleonic era, a Swiss mountain villager must account for the suspicious (though accidental) death of his rival in love. *Sc:* Hans Kräly, from the novel *Der König der Bernina* by Jakob Christoph Heer. *Ph:* Oliver Marsh. *Ed:* Andrew Marton. *Titles:* Katherine Hilliker, H.H. Caldwell. *Mus:* Hugo Riesenthal. *With* John Barrymore *(Marcus Paltram)*, Camilla Horn *(Ciglia)*, Victor Varconi *(Lorenz Gruber)*, Mona Rico *(Pia)*, Hobart Bosworth *(Pastor Tass)*, Bodil Rosing *(Housekeeper)*, Evelyn Selbie *(Pia's Mother)*. *Prod:* Joseph M. Schenk for United Artists. 9 reels. (Lubitsch's last silent film, *Eternal Love* was released with a synchronised sound-effect track, but the film was both a critical and financial failure.)

B. *Sound Films*

THE LOVE PARADE (1929). When a romantic count marries a queen, he finds the usual husband-and-wife rules turned upside-down. In his ample spare time, the Prince Consort balances the kingdom's budget, and finally rebalances the marriage. *Sc:* Ernest Vajda, Guy Bolton, from the play "The Prince Consort" by Leon Xanrof and Jules Chancel. *Ph:* Victor Milner. *Sets:* Hans Dreier. *Ed:* Merrill G. White. *Mus:* Victor Schertzinger. *Lyrics:* Clifford Gray. *Songs:* "Ooh La La," "Paris, Stay the Same," "Dream Lover," "My Love Parade," "Let's Be Common," "Grenadier's Song," "Nobody's Using It Now," "The Queen Is Always Right." *With* Maurice Chevalier *(Count Renard)*, Jeanette MacDonald *(Queen Louise)*, Lupino Lane *(Jacques)*, Lillian Roth *(Lulu)*, Edgar Norton *(Master of Ceremonies)*, Lionel Belmore *(Prime Minister)*, Albert Roccardi *(Foreign Minister)*, Carleton Stockdale *(The Admiral)*, Eugene Pallette *(Minister of War)*, E.H. Calvert *(Sylvanian Ambassador)*, Andre Sheron *(Le Mari)*, Yola D'Avril *(Paulette)*, Margaret Fealy *(First Lady-in-Waiting)*, Virginia Bruce *(Second Lady-in-Waiting)*, Russell Powell *(Afghan Ambassador)*, Winter Hall *(Priest)*, Ben Turpin *(Lackey)*, Jean Harlow (Extra in theatre audience), Anton Vaverka, Albert de Winton, William von Hardenburg, Josephine Hall, Rosalind Charles, Helene Friend. *Prod:* Ernst Lubitsch for Paramount. 12 reels.

PARAMOUNT ON PARADE (1930). Dir: Dorothy Arzner, Otto Brower, Edmund Goulding, Victor Heerman, Edwin Knopf, Rowland Lee, Ernst Lubitsch ("The Origin of the Apache Dance," "A Park In Paris," "Sweeping the Clouds Away"),

Paramount on Parade: Chevalier as a Paris gendarme.

Lothar Mendes, Victor Schertzinger, Edward Sutherland, Frank Tuttle, Charles De Rochefort (European version). *Ph:* Harry Fishbeck, Victor Milner. *Dances:* David Bennett. *Sets:* John Wenger. *Supervisor:* Elsie Janis. *With* Maurice Chevalier *(Lubitsch sequences),* Evelyn Brent *(Chevalier's partner in* "The Origin of the Apache Dance"*),* and (in alphabetical order): Richard Arlen, Jean Arthur, William Austin, George Bancroft, Clara Bow, Mary Brian, Clive Brook, Virginia Bruce, Nancy Carroll, Ruth Chatterton, Gary Cooper, Leon Errol, Stuart Erwin, Kay Francis, Skeets Gallagher, Harry Green, Mitzi Green, James Hall, Phillips Holmes, Helen Kane, Dennis King, Abe Lyman, Fredric March, Nino Martini, Mitzi Mayfair, David Newell, Jack Oakie, Warner Oland, Zelma O'Neill, Eugene Pallette, Joan Peers, William Powell, Charles "Buddy" Rogers, Lillian Roth, Stanley Smith, Fay Wray. *Prod:* Paramount. 102m. (A musical showcase for studio talent, similar to Warner Borthers' *Show of Shows* and M.G.M.'s *Hollywood Revue,* with "a bit more taste than the others" [Huff, p. 20]).

MONTE CARLO (1930). Fleeing from the reality of her circumstances (she is

168

Playing the wheel in *Monte Carlo*.

destitute and on the brink of a marriage for money), the heroine meets and falls in love with a wealthy nobleman whom she believes to be a barber. *Sc:* Ernest Vajda, from the story "The Blue Coast" by Hans Müller, and episodes from "Monsieur Beaucaire" by Booth Tarkington and Evelyn Sutherland. *Add. Dial:* Vincent Lawrence. *Ph:* Victor Milner. *Sets:* Hans Dreier. *Mus:* Richard A. Whiting, Frank Harling. *Lyrics:* Leo Robin. *Songs:* "Give Me a Moment Please," "Always," "Beyond the Blue Horizon," "This Is Something New To Me," "Women, Just Women," "I'm a Simple-Hearted Man," "You'll Love Me and Like It," "Whatever It Is, It's Grand." *With* Jack Buchanan *(Count Rudolph Farriere)*, Jeanette MacDonald *(Countess Helene Mara)*, Zasu Pitts *(Bertha)*, Tyler Brook *(Armand)*, Claude Allister *(Prince Otto von Leibenheim)*, Lionel Belmore *(Duke Gustav von Leibenheim)*, John Roche *(Paul)*, Albert Conti *(Master of Ceremonies)*, Donald Novis *(Monsieur Beaucaire)*, Helen Garden *(Lady Mary)*, David Percy *(Herald)*, Erik Bey *(Lord Winterset)*, Sidney Bracey *(Hunchback)*, Geraldine Dvorak *(Garbo "lookalike" in casino)*. *Prod:* Ernst Lubitsch for Paramount. 90m.

THE SMILING LIEUTENANT (1931). A princess marries a soldier to save her honour (he had "winked" at her). Afterwards she must seek advice from her husband's old flame on how to win his love. *Sc:* Ernest Vajda, Samson Raphaelson, Ernst Lubitsch, from the operetta "The Waltz Dream" by Leopold Jacobson and

169

Maurice Chevalier and Claudette Colbert in *The Smiling Lieutenant*.

The Man I Killed: Phillips Holmes, Louise Cartier, Nancy Carroll, and Lionel Barrymore.

Felix Dormann, and the story "Nux der Prinzgemahl" by Hans Müller. *Ph:* George Folsey. *Sets:* Hans Dreier. *Mus:* Oscar Strauss. *Lyrics:* Clifford Grey. *With* Maurice Chevalier *(Niki)*, Claudette Colbert *(Franzi)*, Miriam Hopkins *(Princess Anna)*, George Barbier *(King Adolf)*, Charles Ruggles *(Max)*, Hugh O'Connell *(Orderly)*, Robert Strange *(Adjutant von Rockoff)*, Janet Reade *(Lily)*, Lon MacSunday *(Emperor)*, Elizabeth Patterson *(Baroness von Schwedel)*, Harry Bradley *(Count von Halden)*, Werner Saxtorph *(Joseph)*, Karl Stall *(Master of Ceremonies)*, Granville Bates *(Bill Collector)*. *Prod:* Ernst Lubitsch for Paramount. 102m.

THE MAN I KILLED (aka Broken Lullaby, 1932). After the First World War, a young Frenchman goes to a German village to confess that he killed the son of the local doctor in battle. Once there, he finds himself taking the dead man's place in the eyes of the family and the dead man's *fiancée*. *Sc:* Ernest Vajda, Samson Raphaelson, from the play by Maurice Rostand, and the English adaptation by Reginald Berkeley. *Ph:* Victor Milner. *Sets:* Hans Dreier. *With* Lionel Barrymore *(Dr. Holderlin)*, Nancy Carroll *(Elsa)*, Phillips Holmes *(Paul)*, Tom Douglas *(Walter Holderlin)*, Zasu Pitts *(Anna)*, Lucien Littlefield *(Schultz)*, Louise Cartier *(Mrs. Holderlin)*, Frank Sheridan *(Priest)*, George Bickel *(Bresslauer)*, Emma Dunn *(Mrs.*

Miller), Tully Marshall *(Gravedigger)*, Lillian Elliott *(Mrs. Bresslauer)*, Marvin Stephans *(Fritz)*, Reginald Pasch *(Fritz's Father)*, Joan Standing *(Flowershop Girl)*, Rodney McKennon *(War Veteran)*, Torben Meyer *(Waiter at Inn)*. *Prod:* Ernst Lubitsch for Paramount. 77m.

ONE HOUR WITH YOU (1932). A musical remake of "The Marriage Circle" (1924), told primarily from the point-of-view of the husband, with the added touch of the hero explaining his perplexities and dilemmas directly to the audience. *Sc:* Samson Raphaelson, from the play "Only a Dream" by Lothar Schmidt. *Ph:* Victor Milner. *Sets:* Hans Dreier. *Dial. Dir:* George Cukor. *Mus:* Oscar Strauss, Richard Whiting. *Lyrics:* Leo Robin. *Songs:* "Mitzi," "What Would You Do?," "One Hour With You," "What a Little Thing Like a Wedding Ring Can Do," "We Will Always Be Sweethearts," "Three Times a Day." *With* Maurice Chevalier *(Dr. André Bertier)*, Jeanette MacDonald *(Colette Bertier)*, Genevieve Tobin *(Mitzi Olivier)*, Charles Ruggles *(Adolphe)*, Roland Young *(Prof. Olivier)*, George Barbier *(Police Commissioner)*, Josephine Dunn *(Mlle. Martell)*, Richard Carle *(Detective)*, Charles Judels *(Policeman)*, Barbara Leonard *(Mitzi's Maid)*. *Prod:* Ernst Lubitsch for Paramount. 9 reels. (Because Lubitsch was still shooting and editing *The Man I Killed,* Paramount assigned George Cukor to direct the script which Lubitsch and Raphaelson had completed. Conflicts with Chevalier and front-office dissatisfaction with the rushes caused Cukor's removal as director. However, Cukor's contract forced him to remain on the set as the nominal "Dialogue Director" while Lubitsch completed the film. Later Cukor had to sue Paramount to keep his name on the credits. [Gavin Lambert, *On Cukor* (New York: Capricorn, 1973), pp. 42-44.])

UNE HEURE PRÈS DE TOI (1932). The French-language version of *One Hour with You. Sc:* Leopold Marchand and André Hornez (translation). Other production and cast credits correspond to the English-language original except that Genevieve Tobin, Roland Young, Charles Ruggles, and George Barbier were replaced, respectively, by Lily Damita, Ernest Ferny, Pierre Etchepare, and André Cheron. 80m.

TROUBLE IN PARADISE (1932). A debonair thief and a beautiful pickpocket fall in love and team up to fleece a glamorous millionairess; jealousy complicates the plot, however, when the thief begins to consider the victim from a romantic rather than professional point-of-view. *Sc:* Samson Raphaelson, from the play "The Honest Finder" by Laszlo Aladar. *Adapt:* Grover Jones. *Ph:* Victor Milner. *Sets:* Hans Dreier. *Mus:* W. Franke Harling. *With* Miriam Hopkins *(Lily)*, Kay Francis *(Marianne)*, Herbert Marshall *(Gaston)*, Charles Ruggles *(The Major)*, Edward Everett Horton *(Francois)*, C. Aubrey Smith *(Giron)*, Robert Grieg *(Jacques, the Butler)*. *Prod:* Ernst Lubitsch for Paramount. 83m. (Together with *The Shop Around the Corner* (1940), one of Lubitsch's two favourite films.)

IF I HAD A MILLION (1932). An omnibus film ringing a series of comic changes on the theme of receiving a million dollar windfall. *Dir:* Ernst Lubitsch ("The Clerk"), James Cruze ("The China Shop"), Stephen Roberts ("The Forger"), Norman McLeod ("The Three Marines"), Bruce Humberstone ("The Condemned Man"), Norman Taurog ("The Auto"), William Seiter ("Old Ladies' Home"). *Sc:* Claude Binyon, Whitney Bolton, Malcom Stuart Boylan, John Bright, Sidney Buchman, Lester Cole, Isabel Dawn, Boyce DeGaw, Walter DeLeon, Oliver H.P. Garrett, Harvey Gates, Grover Jones, Ernst Lubitsch ("The Clerk"), Lawton MacKall, Joseph L. Mankiewicz, William Slavens McNutt, Seton I. Miller, Tiffany

Miriam Hopkins, Gary Cooper, and Fredric March in *Design for Living.*

Thayer, from the story "Windfall" by Robert D. Andrews. *With* Richard Bennett *(The Millionaire); Wynne Gibson (Streetwalker);* Charles Ruggles, Mary Boland ("The China Shop"); George Raft ("The Forger"); Gary Cooper, Jack Oakie, Roscoe Karns, Lucien Littlefield, Joyce Compton ("The Three Marines"); Charles Laughton ("The Clerk"); Francis Dee, Gene Raymond ("The Condemned Man"); Alison Skipworth, W.C. Fields ("The Auto"); May Robson ("Old Ladies' Home"). *Prod:* Paramount. 88m. In "The Clerk" Laughton receives his cheque for a million dollars. He rises from behind his desk (seemingly one among hundreds), climbs several flights of stairs, passes through several doors, until he calmly faces the president of the company. The clerk gives his boss a juicy "raspberry" and exits. Running time: less than three minutes.

DESIGN FOR LIVING (1933). A young American girl in Paris falls in love with two expatriate "artists." After vacillating between the two, she marries a third man, but eventually discovers that she cannot live without either of her bohemian consorts and so decides to live with both, leaving her forlorn husband high and dry. *Sc:* Ben Hecht, from the play by Nöel Coward. *Ph:* Victor Milner. *Art Dir:* Hans Dreier. *Ed:* Francis Marsh. *Mus. Dir:* Nat Finston. *With* Fredric March *(Tom*

Chambers), Gary Cooper *(George Curtis)*, Miriam Hopkins *(Gilda Farrell)*, Edward Everett Horton *(Max Plunkett)*, Franklin Pangborn *(Mr. Douglas)*, Isabel Jewel *(Lisping Secretary)*, Harry Dunkinson *(Mr. Egelbauer)*, Helena Phillips *(Mrs. Egelbauer)*, James Donlin *(Fat Man)*, Vernon Steel *(First Manager)*, Thomas Braidon *(Second Manager)*, Jane Darweli *(Housekeeper)*, Armand Kaliz *(Mr. Burton)*, Adrienne D'Ambricourt *(Café Proprietress)*, Wyndham Standing *(Max's valet)*, Emile Chautard *(Conductor)*, Nora Cecil *(Tom's Secretary)*, George Savidan *(Boy)*, Cosmo Bellew *(Voice of "Bassington")*, Barry Vinton *(Voice of "Edgar")*. *Prod:* Ernst Lubitsch for Paramount. 90m.

MR. BROADWAY (1933). A short film produced and written by Ed Sullivan. Among the celebrities of the time appearing as themselves were Jack Dempsey, Bert Lahr, Joe Frisco, Eddie Duchin, and Ernst Lubitsch. 63m.

THE MERRY WIDOW (1934). The widow Sonia leaves Marshovia for Paris, taking half the kingdom's wealth with her. Captain Danilo is assigned the task of wooing her and bringing her back before the royal treasury defaults. *Sc:* Ernest Vajda, Samson Raphaelson, from the operetta by Victor Leon and Leo Stein. *Ph:* Oliver Marsh. *Art Dir:* Cedric Gibbons. *Cost:* Ali Hubert, Adrian. *Choreo:* Albertina Rasch. *Mus:* Franz Lehar (adapt. by Herbert Stothart). *Lyrics:* Richard Rodgers and Lorenz Hart, Gus Kahn. *With* Maurice Chevalier *(Captain Danilo)*,Jeanette MacDonald *(Sonia)*, Edward Everett Horton *(Ambassador)*, Una Merkel *(Queen Dolores)*, George Barbier *(King Achmed)*, Minna Gombel *(Marcelle)*, Ruth Channing *(Lolo)*, Sterling Holloway *(Orderly)*, Donald Meek *(Valet)*, Herman Bing *(Zizipoff)*, Henry Armetta *(The Turk)*, Akim Tamiroff, Shirley Ross, Barbara Leonard, George Davis, Dorothy Nelson, Eleanor Hunt, Erik Rhoades. *Prod:* Irving Thalberg for Metro-Goldwyn-Mayer. 110m.

LA VEUVE JOYEUSE (1934). The French-language version of *The Merry Widow*. *Sc:* Marcel Achard (translation). *Lyrics:* André Hornez (translation). *With* Maurice Chevalier *(Danilo)*, Jeanette MacDonald *(Sonia)*, Daniele Parola *(Queen Dolores)*, André Berley *(King Achmed)*, Fifi D'Orsay *(Marcelle)*, Marcelle Vallée, Pauline Garon, George Davis, Jean Perry, Albert Petit, Emil Dellys, Georges Renavent, Georgette Rhodes, Anita Pike, Odette Duval, Lya Lys, George Nardelli, Constant Franke, Jacques Venaire, George Renault, Marcel Ventura, Fred Cravens, Sam Ash, Henry Lamont, George de Gombert, Arthur de Ravenne, Fred Malatesta, Georges Colega, Adrienne d'Ambricourt, Eugene Borden, Jules Raucourt, André Cheron, Eugene Beday, Juliet Dika, Carry Daumery, August Tollaire, Gene Gouldeni, Jacques Lory, Andre Ferrier. 114m.

DESIRE (1936). A beautiful jewel thief reforms when she falls in love with the young man who unwittingly helps her to smuggle a stolen necklace into Spain. *Dir:* Frank Borzage. *Sc:* Edwin Justus Mayer, Waldemar Young, Samuel Hoffenstein, from the play "Die schönen Tage von Aranjuez" by Hans Szekely and R.A. Stemmle. *Ph:* Charles Lang, Victor Milner. *Art Dir:* Hans Dreier, Robert Usher. *Ed:* William Shea. *Cost:* Travis Banton. *Special Effects:* Farciot Eduoart, Harry Perry. *Mus:* Frederick Hollander. *Lyrics:* Hollander, Leo Robin. *With* Marlene Dietrich *(Madeleine de Beaupré)*, Gary Cooper *(Tom Bradley)*, John Halliday *(Carlos Margoli)*, William Frawley *(Mr. Gibson)*, Ernest Crossart *(Aristide Duval)*, Akim Tamiroff *(Police Official)*, Alan Mowbray *(Dr. Edouart Pauquet)*, Effie Tilbury *(Aunt Olga)*, Enrique Acosta *(Pedro)*, Alice Feliz *(Pepi)*, Stanley Andrews *(Customs Inspector)*. *Prod:* Ernst Lubitsch for Paramount. 89m. (Produced under Lubitsch's personal supervision while he served as production head of Paramount, 1935-1936.

174

On the *Angel* set: Melvyn Douglas, Marlene Dietrich, and Herbert Marshall.

In this capacity, he also changed the title of Josef von Sternberg's last film with Marlene Dietrich, *Capriccio Espagnole,* to *The Devil Is a Woman* (1935). Lubitsch was planning a re-make of Mauritz Stiller's *Hotel Imperial* (1926) with Dietrich and Charles Boyer, directed by Henry Hathaway, when he was replaced as production chief by William LeBaron, and the film was abandoned).

ANGEL (1937). A former resident of a Parisian "salon" is loved by two men — her husband, a high-ranking politican, who must cope with the knowledge that his "angel" was a prostitute, and her lover, who learns that a prostitute can become an "angel." *Sc:* Samson Raphaelson, from a play by Melchior Lengyel. *Adapt:* Guy Bolton, Russell Medcraft. *Ph:* Charles Lang. *Art Dir:* Hans Dreier, Robert Usher. *Ed:* William Shea. *Special Effects:* Farciot Edouart. *Cost:* Travis Banton. *Mus:* Frederick Hollander. *Lyrics:* Leo Robin. *Mus. Dir:* Boris Morros. *With* Marlene Dietrich *(Lady Maria Barker),* Herbert Marshall *(Sir Frederick Barker),* Melvyn Douglas *(Anthony Halton),* Edward Everett Horton *(Graham),* Ernest Crossart *(Walton),* Laura Hope Crews *(Grand Duchess Anna Dmitrievna),* Herbert Mundin *(Greenwood),* Ivan Lebedeff *(Prince Vladimir Gregorovitch),* Dennie Moore *(Emma),* Lionel Pape *(Lord Davington),* Phyllis Coghlen *(Maid),* Leonard Caret *(First Footman),* Eric Wilton *(English Chauffeur),* Gerald Hamer *(Second Footman),* Herbert Evans *(Butler),* Michael Visaroff *(Russian Butler),* Olaf Hytten *(Photographer),* Duci Kerekjarto, Sam Harris. *Prod:* Ernst Lubitsch for Paramount. 98m.

BLUEBEARD'S EIGHTH WIFE (1938). Bluebeard's eighth wife is determined that she will be his last — and drives him to the sanitorium to prove her point. *Sc:* Charles Brackett, Billy Wilder, from a play by Alfred Savior. *Adapt:* Charlton Andrews. *Ph:* Leo Tover. *Art Dir:* Hans Dreier, Robert Usher. *Ed:* William Shea. *Special Effects:* Farciot Edouart. *Cost:* Travis Banton. *Mus:* Werner R. Heyman. *With* Claudette Colbert *(Nicole de Loiselle),* Gary Cooper *(Michael Brandon),* Edward Everett Horton *(Marquis de Loiselle),* David Niven *(Albert de Régnier),* Elizabeth Patterson *(Aunt Hedwige),* Herman Bing *(Pepinard),* Warren Hymer *(Kid Mulligan),* Franklin Pangborn *(Assistant Hotel Manager),* Armand Cortes *(Assistant Hotel Manager),* Rolfe Sedan *(Floor-walker),* Lawrence Grant *(Prof. Urganzeff),* Lionel Pape *(Potin),* Tyler Brooke *(Clerk),* Tom Ricketts *(Uncle André),* Barlow Borland *(Uncle Fernandel),* Charles Halton, Sacha Guitry. *Prod:* Ernst Lubitsch for Paramount. 80m.

NINOTCHKA (1939). Sent to Paris on a diplomatic mission, a cold-blooded Communist meets a fast-talking gigolo who depends for his livelihood on the favours of an exiled Grand Duchess. They fall in love, Ninotchka learns how to laugh, and her lover becomes his own man. *Sc:* Charles Brackett, Billy Wilder, Walter Reisch, from an original story by Melchior Lengyel. *Ph:* William Daniels. *Art Dir:* Cedric Gibbons, Randall Duel, Edwin B. Willis. *Ed:* Gene Ruggiero. *Cost:* Adrian. *Mus:* Werner R. Heymann. *With* Greta Garbo *(Ninotchka),* Melvyn Douglas *(Leon),* Ina Clair *(Swana),* Bela Lugosi *(Razinin),* Felix Bressart *(Buljanoff),* Alexander Granach *(Kopalski),* Gregory Gay *(Rakonin),* Rolfe Sedan *(Hotel Manager),* Edwin Maxwell *(Mercier),* Richard Carle *(Gaston),* Sig Rumann *(Iranoff),* George Tobias, Paul Ellis, Dorothy Adams, Peggy Moran. *Prod:* Ernst Lubitsch for Metro-Goldwyn-Mayer. 110m.

THE SHOP AROUND THE CORNER (1940). In pre-war Budapest, two shop clerks, who cannot stand each other at work, unwittingly carry on a courtship by mail. At the same time, the shopowner's suspicion that the young man is having an affair with his wife drives him to the brink of suicide. The film ends happily with the major problems appropriately resolved on Christmas Eve. *Sc:* Samson

That Uncertain Feeling: **Burgess Meredith and Merle Oberon discuss modern art.**

Raphaelson, from a play by Nikolaus Laszlo. *Ph:* William Daniels. *Art Dir:* Cedric Gibbons, Wade B. Rubottom, Edwin B. Willis. *Ed:* Gene Ruggiero. *Mus:* Werner R. Heymann. *With* Margaret Sullavan *(Klara Novak),* James Stewart *(Alfred Kralik),* Frank Morgan *(Hugo Matuschek),* Joseph Schildkraut *(Ferencz Vadas),* Sara Haden *(Flora),* Felix Bressart *(Pirovitch),* William Tracy *(Pepi Katona),* Inez Courtney *(Ilona),* Sarah Edwards *(Customer),* Edwin Maxwell *(Doctor),* Charles Halton *(Detective),* Charles Smith *(Rudy). Prod:* Ernst Lubitsch for Metro-Goldwyn-Mayer. 97m.

THAT UNCERTAIN FEELING (1941). A remake of *Kiss Me Again,* updated and set in New York, in order to satirize psychoanalysis and bohemian artists. *Sc:* Donald Ogden Stewart, from the play "Nous divorcons" by Victorien Sardou and Emile de Najac. *Adapt:* Walter Reisch. *Ph:* George Barnes. *Art Dir:* Alexander Golitzen. *Ed:* William Shea. *Cost:* Irene. *Assts:* Horace Hough, Lee Scholem. *Mus:* Werner R. Heymann. *With* Merle Oberon *(Jill Baker),* Melvyn Douglas *(Larry Baker),* Burgess Meredith *(Sebastian),* Alan Mowbray *(Dr. Vengard),* Olive Blakeney

(Margie Stallings), Harry Davenport *(Jones)*, Eve Arden *(Sally)*, Sig Rumann *(Kafka)*, Richard Carle *(Butler)*, Mary Currier *(Maid)*, Jean Fenwick *(Nurse)*. *Prod:* Ernst Lubitsch for United Artists. 84m.

TO BE OR NOT TO BE (1942). In Warsaw during the Nazi *blitzkrieg*, a troupe of actors scheme and counter-scheme to outwit the Gestapo, while at the same time the harried and egocentric "star" attempts to cope with his equally egotistic (and flirtatious) co-star-wife. The actors succeed in outwitting the Germans. *Sc:* Edwin Justus Mayer, from an original story by Ernst Lubitsch and Melchior Lengyel. *Ph:* Rudolph Maté. *Art Dir:* Vincent Korda. *Ed:* Dorothy Spencer. *Cost:* Irene. *Assts:* William Tummel, William McGarry. *Mus:* Werner R. Heymann. *With* Carole Lombard *(Maria Tura)*, Jack Benny *(Joseph Tura)*, Robert Stack *(Lt. Stanislav Sobinsky)*, Felix Bressart *(Greenberg)*, Lionel Atwill *(Rawitch)*, Stanley Ridges *(Prof. Siletsky)*, Sig Rumann *(Col. Ehrhardt)*, Tom Dugan *(Bronski)*, Charles Halton *(Dobosh)*, George Lynn *(Actor-Adjutant)*, Henry Victor *(Capt. Schultz)*, Maude Eburne *(Anna)*, Armand Wright *(Make-up Man)*, Erno Verebes *(Stage Manager)*, Halliwell Hobbes *(Gen. Armstrong)*, Miles Mander *(Maj. Cunningham)*, Leslie Dennison *(Captain)*, Frank Reicher *(Polish Official)*, Peter Caldwell *(William Kunze)*, Wolfgang Zilzer *(Man in Bookstore)*, Olaf Hytten *("Polonius" in Warsaw)*, Charles Irwin *(Reporter)*, Leland Hodgson *(Second Reporter)*, Alec Craig *(Scottish Farmer)*, James Finlayson *(Second Farmer)*, Edgar Licho *(Prompter)*, Robert O. Davis *(Gestapo Sergeant)*, Roland Varno *(Pilot)*, Helmut Dantine, Otto Reichow *(Co-Pilots)*, Maurice Murphy, Gene Rizzi, Paul Barrett, John Kellogg *(Polish R.A.F. Flyers)*. *Prod:* Ernst Lubitsch and Alexander Korda for United Artists. 99m.

HEAVEN CAN WAIT (1943). In the vestibule of Hades an old man recounts his "sinful" life to the gatekeeper: a life of steadfast love for his wife despite a paradoxically innocent string of philanderings. With the warning that "there's no room for your kind down here," he is sent to apply "upstairs." *Sc:* Samson Raphaelson, from the play "Birthday" by Lazlo Bus-Feketé. *Ph:* Edward Cronjager (Technicolor.). *Art Dir:* James Basevi, Leland Fuller, Thomas Little, Walter M. Scott. *Ed:* Dorothy Spencer. *Technicolor Colour Consultant:* Natalie Kalmus. *Special Effects:* Fred Sersen. *Cost:* Rene Hubert. *Asst:* Henry Weinberger. *Mus:* Alfred Newman. *With* Gene Tierney *(Martha)*, Don Ameche *(Henry Van Cleve)*, Charles Coburn *(Hugo Van Cleve)*, Laird Cregar *(His Excellency)*, Spring Byington *(Bertha Van Cleve)*, Allen Joslyn *(Albert Van Cleve)*, Marjorie Main *(Mrs. Strabel)*, Eugene Pallette *(E. F. Strabel)*, Signe Hasso *("Mademoiselle")*, Louis Calhern *(Randolph Van Cleve)*, Helene Reynolds *(Peggy Nash)*, Aubrey Mather *(James)*, Michael Ames *(Jack Van Cleve)*, Clarence Muse *(Jasper)*, Scotty Beckett *(Henry, aged seven)*, Dickie Moore *(Henry, aged fifteen)*, Dickie Jones *(Albert, aged fifteen)*, Trudy Marshall *(Jane)*, Florence Bates *(Edna Craig)*, Clara Blandick *(Grandmother)*, Anita Bolster *(Mrs. Cooper-Cooper)*, Nino Pipitone Jr. *(Jack, as a Boy)*, Claire du Brey *(Miss Ralston)*, Maureen Rodin-Ryan *(Nurse)*. *Prod:* Ernst Lubitsch for 20th Century-Fox. 112m.

A ROYAL SCANDAL (1945). A remake of *Forbidden Paradise* (1924). Lubitsch suffered a heart attack shortly after production began. The film was completed by Otto Preminger. *Dir:* Otto Preminger. *Sc:* Edwin Justus Mayer, from the play "The Czarina" by Lajos Biro and Melchior Lengyel. *Adapt:* Bruno Frank. *Ph:* Arthur Miller. *Art Dir:* Lyle Wheeler. *Ed:* Dorothy Spencer. *Special Effects:* Fred Sersen. *Cost:* Rene Hubert. *Asst:* Tom Dudley. *Mus:* Alfred Newman. *With* Tallulah Bankhead *(The Czarina)*, Charles Coburn *(The Chancellor)*, Anne Baxter *(Anna)*, William Eythe *(Alexei)*, Vincent Price *(Marquis de Fleury)*, Mischa Auer *(Capt. Sukov)*, Sig Rumann *(Gen. Ronsky)*, Vladimir Sokoloff *(Malakoff)*, Mikhail Rasumny *(Drunken General)*, Grady Sutton *(Boris)*, Don Douglas *(Variatinsky)*,

Eva Gabor *(Countess Demidow)*, Egon Brecher *(Wassilikow)*. *Prod:* Ernst Lubitsch for 20th Century-Fox. 94m.

WHERE DO WE GO FROM HERE? (1945). *Dir:* Gregory Ratoff. *Sc:* Morrie Ryskind, from a story by Ryskind and Sig Herzig. *Ph:* Leon Shamroy (Technicolor). *Art Dir:* Lyle Wheeler, Leland Fuller, Thomas Little, Walter M. Scott. *Ed:* J. Watson Webb. *Technicolor Colour Consultants:* Natalie Kalmus, Richard Mueller. *Special Effects:* Fred Sersen. *Choreo:* Fanchon. *Mus:* David Raksin. *Lyrics:* Kurt Weill, Ira Gershwin. *With* Fred MacMurray, Joan Leslie, June Haver, Gene Sheldon, Anthony Quinn, Carlos Ramirez, Alan Mowbray, Fortunio Bonanova, Herman Bing, Howard Freeman, John Davidson, Rosina Galli, Fred Essler, Ernst Lubitsch, Otto Preminger. *Prod:* William Perlberg for 20th Century-Fox. 77m. (Lubitsch reputedly played a bit-part as a mutinous sailor on Christopher Columbus's ship. [Weinberg, p. 334]).

DRAGONWYCK (1946). Reminiscent of "Jane Eyre" but set in the Hudson River valley in the 1840's, this melodrama is about a young governess's growing fascination with the moody and autocratic Dutch landowner who employs her. *Dir:* Joseph L. Mankiewicz. *Sc:* Mankiewicz, from the novel by Anya Seton. *Ph:* Arthur Miller. *Art Dir:* Lyle Wheeler, J. Russell Spencer, Thomas Little, Paul S. Fox. *Ed:* Dorothy Spencer. *Special Effects:* Fred Sersen. *Cost:* Rene Hubert. *Choreo:* Arthur Appel. *Mus:* Alfred Newman. *With* Gene Tierney *(Miranda Wells)*, Walter Huston *(Ephraim Wells)*, Vincent Price *(Nicholas van Ryn)*, Glenn Langan *(Dr. Jeff Turner)*, Anne Revere *(Abigail Wells)*, Spring Byington *(Magda)*, Connie Marshall *(Katrine van Ryn)*, Henry Morgan *(Bleecker)*, Vivienne Osborne *(Johanna van Ryn)*, Jessica Tandy *(Peggy O'Malley)*, Trudy Marshall *(Elisabeth van Borden)*, David Ballard *(Obadiah)*, Scott Elliott *(Tom Wells)*, Boyd Irwin *(Tompkins)*, Maya van Horn *(Countess de Grenier)*, Keith Hitchcock *(Mr. MacNabb)*, Francis Pierlot *(A Doctor)*, Tom Fadden *(Otto)*, Grady Sutton *(Hotel Employee)*. *Prod:* Ernst Lubitsch for 20th Century-Fox. 103m.

CLUNY BROWN (1946). An intellectual European war-refugee initiates an upper-class British family into the realities of the world beyond their garden wall, while one of their servants destroys her chance to marry into the middle-class because she would rather fix the plumbing than ignore it. When the two decide they love each other, they emigrate to America, to pursue their true vocations – she to be wife and plumber, he to be husband and author of best-selling mystery novels. *Sc:* Samuel Hoffenstein, Elizabeth Reinhardt, from the novel by Margery Sharp. *Ph:* Joseph La Shelle. *Art Dir:* Lyle Wheeler, J. Russell Spencer. *Ed:* Dorothy Spencer. *Special Effects:* Fred Sersen. *Cost:* Bonnie Cashin. *Asst:* Tom Dudley. *Mus:* Cyril Mockridge. *Mus Dir:* Emil Newman. *With* Charles Boyer *(Adam Belinsky)*, Jennifer Jones *(Cluny Brown)*, Peter Lawford *(Andrew Carmel)*, Helen Walker *(Betty Cream)*, Reginald Gardiner *(Hilary Ames)*, Reginald Owen *(Sir Henry Carmel)*, Sir C. Aubrey Smith *(Col. Duff Graham)*, Richard Haydn *(Wilson)*, Margaret Bannerman *(Lady Alice Carmel)*, Sara Allgood *(Mrs. Maile)*, Ernest Crossart *(Syrette)*, Florence Bates *(Dowager)*, Una O'Connor *(Mrs. Wilson)*, Queenie Leonard *(Weller)*, Billy Bevan *(Uncle Arn)*, Michael Dyne *(John Frewen)*, Christopher Severn *(Master Snaffle)*, Rex Evans *(Guest Pianist)*, Ottola Nesmith *(Mrs. Tupham)*, Harold De Becker *(Mr. Snaffle)*, Jean Prescott *(Mrs. Sniffle)*, Al Winters *(Rollins)*, Clive Morgan *(Waiter)*, Charles Coleman *(Constable Birkins)*, George Kirby *(Latham)*, Whitner Bissell *(Dowager's Son)*, Betty Rae Brown *(Girl at Party)*, Mira McKinney *(Author's Wife)*, Philip Morris *(Policeman)*, Betty Fairfax *(Woman in Chemist's Shop)*, Norman Ainsley *(Mr. Tupham)*. *Prod:* Ernst Lubitsch for 20th Century-Fox. 100m.

THE LADY IN ERMINE (1948). With the help of her ghostly ancestors, the Countess of Bergamo negotiates peace between Bergamo and Hungary; and she proves her sincerity by dumping her cowardly husband for the Hungarian Colonel who captures both her castle and her heart. *Sc:* Samson Raphaelson, from an operetta by Rudolf Schanzer and E. Welische. *Ph:* Leon Shamroy (Technicolor). *Art Dir:* Lyle Wheeler, J. Russell Spencer. *Ed:* Dorothy Spencer. *Technicolor Colour Consultants:* Natalie Kalmus, Leonard Doss. *Special Effects:* Fred Sersen. *Cost:* Rene Hubert. *Asst:* Tom Dudley. *Choreo:* Hermes Pan. *Mus:* Alfred Newman. *Lyrics:* Leo Robin, Frederick Hollander. *Songs:* "This Is the Moment," "There's Something About the Midnight," "Ooh What I'll Do." *With* Betty Grable *(Francesca and Angelina),* Douglas Fairbanks Jr. *(Col. Ladislaus Karoly Teglash and The Duke of Ravenna),* Cesar Romero *(Mario),* Walter Abel *(Maj. Horvath and Benevenuto),* Reginald Gardiner *(Alberto),* Harry Davenport *(Luigi),* Virginia Campbell *(Theresa),* Whit Bissell *(Giulio),* Edmund MacDonald *(Capt. Novak),* David Bond *(Gabor),* Harry Cording, Belle Mitchell, Mary Bear, Jack George, John Parrish, Mayo Newhall *(Six Ancestors),* Lester Allen *(Jester). Prod:* Ernst Lubitsch for 20th Century-Fox. 89m. (After less than two weeks of shooting, Ernst Lubitsch suffered a heart attack; he died on 30 November 1947. Otto Preminger finished the film, but sole directorial credit was given to Lubitsch.)

IN THE GOOD OLD SUMMERTIME (1949). Musical remake of *The Shop Around the Corner. Dir:* Robert Z. Leonard. *Sc:* Albert Hackett, Francis Goodrich, Ivan Tors, based on the screenplay by Samson Raphaelson and the play by Miklos Laszlo. *With* Judy Garland, Van Johnson, S. Z. Sakall, Spring Byington, Buster Keaton.

SILK STOCKINGS (1957). Film version of a stage musical based upon *Ninotchka* (1939). *Dir:* Rouben Mamoulian. *Sc:* Leonard Gershe, Leonard Spiegelglass, from the play by George S. Kauffman, Leueen McGrath and Abe Burrows based upon the screenplay by Charles Brackett, Billy Wilder and Walter Reisch and the story by Melchior Lengyel. *Ph:* Robert Bronner (Cinemascope/Metrocolor). *Art Dir:* William A. Horning, Randall Duell, Edwin B. Willis, Hugh Hunt. *Ed:* Harold F. Kress. *Cost:* Helen Rose. *Music and Lyrics:* Cole Porter. *Mus Dir:* André Previn. *Choreo:* Hermes Pan, Eugene Loring. *With* Fred Astaire *(Steve Canfield),* Cyd Charisse *(Ninotchka),* Janis Paige *(Peggy Dainton),* Peter Lorre *(Brankov),* Jules Munshin *(Bibinski),* Joseph Buloff *(Ivanov),* George Tobias *(Commissar),* Wim Sonneveld *(Peter Ilyitch Boroff),* Belita *(Dancer),* Ivan Triesault *(Russian Embassy Official),* Betty Utti, Tybee Afra, Barrie Chase *(Dancers). Prod:* Arthur Freed for Metro-Goldwyn-Mayer. 117m.